SOMEONE TO BELIEVE IN

SOMEONE TO BELIEVE IN

EMBRACING THE SAVIOR WHO STAYS THE SAME WHEN EVERYTHING ELSE CHANGES

COURTNEY REISSIG

PUBLISHING®
BRENTWOOD, TENNESSEE

Printed in the United States of America

979-8-3845-1185-4

Published by B&H Publishing Group
Brentwood, Tennessee

Dewey Decimal Classification: 234.2
Subject Heading: FAITH / BELIEF AND DOUBT /
CHRISTIAN LIFE

Cover design by Lindy Kasler. Cover images "Tree in a Landscape" by John Kelt Edwards, from the National Library of Wales (Public Domain). Fandorina Liza and Jan Wachowski/Shutterstock.
Author photo by Lydia Singleton.

1 2 3 4 5 6 • 28 27 26 25

For the ones who wonder if he's believable.

He is.

Contents

Introduction: The Times Are Changing 1

Part 1: The Same in the Past

Chapter 1: He Has Come to Rescue Us (John 1–2). 13

Chapter 2: He Has Not Been Impressed by Your Religion (John 3). 29

Chapter 3: He Has Covered Your Past Shame (John 4). 49

Chapter 4: Living Water Reshapes My Identity 67

Part 2: The Same in the Present

Chapter 5: He Is Not Disappointing You (John 9–10) 81

Chapter 6: He Is with You (John 13–16). 101

Chapter 7: He Is Praying for You (John 17). 119

Chapter 8: His Presence Restores My Trust. 139

Part 3: The Same in the Future

Chapter 9: He Will Provide for You (John 6) 151

Chapter 10: He Will End All Suffering (John 11) 169

Chapter 11: He Will Make a Home for You (John 14) 187

Chapter 12: The Bread of Life Gives Me Hope 205

Conclusion: The Stability of Our Times 215

Acknowledgments 223

Notes 225

INTRODUCTION

The Times Are Changing

"I don't trust Christians. They're all hypocrites."

"God never answers my prayers. I'm giving up."

"The Bible has contradictions. I'm not wasting my time on it anymore."

"My suffering is too much. God can't be trusted."

"My doubts are too heavy. I'm walking away."

THESE ARE ALL STATEMENTS Molly heard over the years in her ministry to young adults and young married couples. For two decades, she sat with people as they planned funerals for children. She heard spouses' stories of infidelity and breeches of trust. She counseled people through job losses and financial turmoil. And one day she had to listen to a young mom explain through tears that Jesus no longer seemed trustworthy. This mom lived through her childhood pastor's moral failing, her parents' divorce, and now her husband's doubts about his own faith.

"The Bible just doesn't add up for me anymore. I've met friends who can make sense of life without God in it, and honestly, that is easier," she said.

After months of meeting, this mom finished her final counseling session with Molly and resigned her membership. A few years later, Molly saw her at a football game with her son. She was no longer in church, but didn't seem any more satisfied than during those days on the couch in her office. She was still seeking answers, but couldn't darken a church doorstep anymore. "Too much time has passed," she said, "I'm too busy now, and I don't see Christians acting any different today than they did back then."

Over the years in ministry, I have heard many stories like Molly's. Heart-wrenching stories. Stories that make a person double over in grief. Stories that have led dearly loved friends to resign themselves in battle, beaten down by the enemy one too many times. And due to those stories, I've watched people walk away from not just organized religion, but Jesus.

And yet I've also seen people fight for faith when nothing seemed hopeful around them. I've walked with people who have faced grief and disappointment to no end, and have somehow emerged from the ashes burned, but not incinerated—their faith in God deepened through suffering. When all around their soul gave way, Christ was all their "hope and stay," as the old hymn goes.[1]

For my husband and me, the early days of ministry seemed limitless, with nothing but possibilities and good work to be done in Jesus's name. With nothing but growth ahead for ourselves and everyone around us. I suppose we've been in ministry long enough now, though, that we've watched the parable of the soils play out before our eyes. Good work was indeed to be done and headed our way, but just as the Scriptures promise, so was drought and storm. Seasons of inclement weather have blown through our lives, and now as we look up, we've noticed a great many changes to the landscape around us, particularly when it comes to the company we've kept over the years. Just recently, we reflected on the people we once worshipped alongside who no longer dare come near a church. And we also stand beside people every Sunday who've been through a few battles alongside us.

Molly's friend and my friends who have wrestled deeply with their faith—they aren't alone. Over the years, I too have asked questions into the night, wondering if God was still there.

Perhaps you're asking questions as well. You want to keep hanging on, but don't know what you're grasping for. Or maybe this isn't your struggle, but you're walking alongside someone asking these questions.

Where do you go when all that was once stabilizing suddenly shifts underneath you? Do you walk away like Molly's friend? Or do you keep looking for answers to your doubts? When the circumstances of life push you back against the wall of your faith, do you walk out the door, or do you stay?

A few years ago, I found myself in a season where my world felt like it was crumbling. Many of the things I thought I knew were no longer true. I was in a new place, making new friends, and starting new rhythms. It was disorienting. I tried so hard to grasp for something familiar, something—anything—safe. But grabbing for stability was like grasping for a feather. It was in view, but the minute I got close to it, it blew away again.

My soul begged for stability, but everywhere I turned it was elusive. My heart longed for rest, but chaos swirled around me. I needed steadying, but it wasn't coming from within.

Our pastor at the time was preaching through Hebrews, and as he neared the end of the series this verse washed over me like a torrent of water in a parched land:

> Jesus Christ is the same yesterday, today, and forever. (Heb. 13:8)

Have you ever gone to church one Sunday and sensed the Lord delivering a word from the Scriptures straight into your heart? Straight into your circumstances? Sitting in that pew Sunday morning, I knew he was doing just that for me. A lot of things felt shaky, but the unchanging nature of Jesus Christ was the anchor I was looking for. It was time to learn what it meant to not just agree mentally with this truth about Jesus, but grab onto it for dear life as the world gave way.

It took some time, but I can say with conviction that I've learned what it means to be steadied and stabilized in days of upheaval. Not by a new season or a better set of circumstances, mind you, but by Christ unchangeable. On that random Sunday morning when everything around me seemed to be shifting, I desperately needed to grasp onto the Savior who stays steady. And I've needed to do the same countless times since. As they say, the times are always changing. My life is always changing. My circumstances are regularly uncertain, but Jesus never is. This has become the repeated refrain of my life when I need someone to believe in and all the people around me seem untrustworthy. When *my* times keep changing.

There are a lot of things that lead people to believe this promise in Hebrews can't be true. One of those things tends to be people who let us down. People who were supposed to be like Jesus, maybe. People who were supposed to guide us, perhaps. Or people who were at least supposed to care.

I've been there. Perhaps you're there right now.

What's striking about the location of this Hebrews passage is that it comes right after the exhortation to remember your leaders—the ones "who have spoken God's word to you" (Heb. 13:7). Why do we need reminding that Jesus stays the same—right after hearing about our spiritual leaders?

Just scan recent history (or all of history, really) to find out the reason. Leaders fall all the time. Those charged with caring for us disappoint us on the regular. Even the best men and women succumb to their fallen nature from time to time. When we look at the church landscape today, we hear of Christians deconstructing quite frequently. We learn of people doubting their faith because of unbelief in God's Word, disappointment from church leaders, or even their own sin.

Deconstructing is a buzzword today. For some, it means turning from their faith in Christ entirely. For others, it means untangling their experience of faith from what the Bible says is true. Some deconstruct and come out an atheist. Others deconstruct to a stronger faith in Christ alone. No matter the outcome, the impetus for reexamining your faith can often be identified either in an event or a lifetime of micro-events.

Maybe for you, it's not people. Maybe it's physical suffering, or wondering when you'll get your next paycheck, or the ache of loneliness when everyone around you seems to have found both their soulmate *and* a flourishing friend group. Or maybe your struggle with unbelief isn't visible. Your life is comfortable. You've walked the narrow road. But in the quietness of your mind, unbelief lurks, questioning what you hold close. However you experience it, the common denominator is this: you feel shaky. Like the ground beneath you is fracturing. Like the landscape around you is changing, be it slow or fast, and nothing looks quite the same as it used to. Your footing is off, and with it, your heading in life. We might not have the same experience that led to the shifting foundation, but we all know uncertainty when it creeps up on us.

And yet, *Jesus Christ is the same yesterday, today, and forever.*

The reality of our Savior's unchanging character stabilizes us in a world of rocky terrain.

> When we hear news of another Christian walking away from the faith or falling into moral failure—*Jesus Christ is the same yesterday, today, and forever.*
>
> When we get a hard diagnosis or endure a long-term illness—*Jesus stays the same.*

> When we experience sleepless nights or long days that can't seem to find a groove—*Jesus stays the same.*
>
> When our marriages face trouble, or our jobs are hard—*Jesus stays the same.*
>
> When there is disunity in our churches or confusion about whom to trust—*Jesus stays the same.*
>
> When long-time leaders prove themselves untrustworthy or change their minds on a dime—*Jesus stays the same.*
>
> When we believed in someone who not only waffled in their commitment to us, but failed us—*Jesus Christ stays the same.*
>
> When full-force, cultural winds of change tear through our ethical landscape and our society can no longer tell up from down or right from wrong—*Jesus Christ stays the same.*
>
> When doubts about our faith assail us—*Jesus Christ stays the same.*

We all have a story to share about how life shatters us. But if we trust in Jesus, we all have a testimony to give about his unchanging nature giving us the strength to pick up the pieces—or not be broken beyond repair. If we are going to stand in the shifting sand of life, we need to know this concrete Savior. Things may change, and we may change, but knowing that he doesn't sustains us. He's worth believing in.

That is where we're headed. This book is divided into three parts. Each section is an attempt to give tools to remove the barriers to belief that currently stand in our way. Part 1 looks at Jesus from the vantage point of our past. In chapter 1, we will see how he came to rescue us. He has no beginning and no end, but he invaded time and space to bring us back. For some, our own efforts and religious fervor are barriers to our belief. For others, we can't see an out from our past shame. Chapters 2 and 3 speak to both the saint and the sinner. To the saint, Jesus is not impressed; to the sinner, he's not afraid. Every part of the book wraps up with a story of real-life belief. The fight for faith is best done alongside fellow sojourners, so I've invited others to share their stories in the hopes that you will see theirs in yours—and you will grasp on to belief as they speak to their own.

Part 2 unpacks all the ways Jesus is the same in our present. In chapter 5, we answer the prevailing question of our current cultural moment—is Jesus trustworthy when earthly shepherds aren't? We've likely all walked through seasons of doubt, so we will look at the promise of his presence in chapter 6 and the comfort of his intercession in chapter 7.

We wrap up in part 3 with Jesus's believability for our future. How we trust in the present is directly tied to our future hope. In chapter 9, we look at the Bread of Life in John 6, who shows us that he's the best bread and in him we will never ache for sustenance again. Chapter 10 speaks to the hope Jesus provides to grieving people. In chapter 11, Jesus shows incredible comfort as the one who makes a home for his children. No matter your earthly home, a better one is coming.

Consider the Source

In every encounter with Jesus in this book, I hope you walk away with this strong anchor—Jesus Christ is bigger and stronger than your barriers to belief. Do you want to know how Jesus Christ stays the same, that he's someone to believe in? Go directly to the ones who walked with him.

Throughout the Gospels, we have a clear picture of Jesus. These eyewitness accounts are gathered from men who walked with him. The ones who saw his miracles. The ones who heard his words. Even the ones (like John) who witnessed *both* his death and resurrection. We could look at any of the Gospels to get a clear picture of the Savior, but I find John's account most compelling. Why? Because he is desperate for us to have someone to believe in.

John's Gospel is divided into what is known as "The Book of Signs" (John 1–11), which is the day-to-day ministry of Jesus, and "The Book of Glory" (John 11–21), which reveals the final days of the Savior. Both of these sections work toward one intended purpose that John himself makes clear in chapter 20:31 (ESV):

> These things are written so that you may believe that Jesus is the Christ, the Son of God, and that by believing you may have life in his name.

Everything in John's Gospel was written with this singular purpose in mind. The word *believe* is used ninety-eight times in John, which is significantly more than any of the Synoptic Gospel writers.[2] The other Gospel writers were concerned with belief, but that wasn't their main objective. But it was John's. He didn't compile his Gospel just because he liked these stories the best. He had a clear purpose—*believe in Jesus*. Everything he writes about Jesus demands a response—and in that response we live. So, every time we read a story in John's Gospel, we should be asking, "How is this leading to belief? And how is this leading to life?" The implication of belief is trust and conviction that Jesus is who he says he is. This leads to life-altering discipleship.

When we try to make sense of life in a broken world, the ground beneath us shifts. But when we look long and hard at Jesus Christ, the Son of the living God, we stabilize.

When it comes to uncertainty, unbelief creeps in. When it comes to church hurt, we equate the failure of the church with the Savior. When we can't see the outcome, we wonder if God is still working for our good. When it comes to suffering, we think God has forgotten us. But this is where Hebrews 13:8 connects to John 20:31. If Jesus Christ doesn't change, then we have everything we need to believe in him. And no matter what life throws at us, he is worthy of our belief. Said another way, in an ever-changing world with its ever-changing characters, Jesus *can't* change on us. This is precisely why he's worth believing in over everything else we were believing in before.

In his Gospel, John points us to the Messiah who is utterly in control of his destiny—he is the resurrection and the life. He points us to the Shepherd who is compassionate and relentless in his pursuit of lost people. He points us to the Bread of Life, who is mighty to save, holds all power to heal, and is everything we need. But John doesn't only want us to witness these traits of Christ, *he wants us to believe them*. To bank on them. To live like they're true and they'll never change. To be steadied by them when the ground cracks open and the winds pick up.

It's not enough to just give mental assent to what you hear and read about Jesus. John says that your belief must change your expectations and your reality.

If Jesus is the same yesterday, today, and forever, then it serves us well to see how he is the same from beginning to end too. Not just for all of Christian history, but in our individual histories too.

Let's look at this unchanging Christ together, friends. As we peer through John's lens, let's find Jesus to be exactly who he says he is: someone to believe in.

PART 1

THE SAME IN THE PAST

1

He Has Come to Rescue Us

(John 1–2)

In the book *BEFORE You Lose Your Faith*, Trevin Wax writes about what he calls "two categories of doubt." He says, "The first set focuses on the *veracity* of Christian teaching: *Is Christianity true?*" He goes on to write, "The second set of doubts focuses on the *goodness* of Christian teaching: *Is Christianity good?*"[1] The premise is there are two camps people fall into when they're tempted to walk away from this historic faith delivered to the saints. One group sees the truth claims of Jesus as untenable for belief. The things Jesus claims about himself, and that others claim about him, feel forced and impossible. Doubt creeps in when you try to fit Christianity into a box.

The other end sees the sweeping struggles in the church today as proof that our faith is not sustainable. Leaders fail morally, Christians backbite one another, hypocrites are in every pew, all pointing to a culture that is far from good. Doubt creeps in when people who claim the name of Christ fail to act like him.

In John 1, we are up against the former: *Is Christianity true?* All other Gospel writers begin with the time around or right after Jesus's birth. Matthew begins with a genealogy and gets right to the manger scene. Mark wastes no time launching Jesus into ministry in adulthood. Luke lingers in the family of Jesus, introducing us to Elizabeth and Zechariah and his cousin, John the Baptist.

But John runs in an entirely different direction.

Remember, John's primary point in this Gospel is found in John 20:31—he not only wants us to ponder his account of Jesus; he wants us to *believe* Jesus. He wants us to see who Christ is and find him worthy of our belief. If he ends the book with his purpose statement, he begins the book with where he is headed.

The first eighteen verses of John 1 are stacked with themes that will be revisited repeatedly in the Gospel of John. He leaves clues, words, and markers that we can hang our hats on as we journey throughout this Gospel account. In fact, these first verses are called the "Prologue." It's the introduction to the entire book, and in this introduction, John takes us on a journey that the other Gospel writers allude to, but do not unpack.

In the Beginning

John begins with familiar words. "In the beginning." John assumes his readers have an awareness of the Old Testament, and even a novice Bible student hears echoes of Genesis 1:1. But there is a slight variation. In Genesis 1, Moses writes, "In the beginning God created the heavens and the earth." But in John 1, we read:

> In the beginning was the Word, and the Word was with God, and the Word was God. He was with God in the beginning. All things were created through him, and apart from him not one thing was created that has been created. (vv. 1–3)

In Genesis we see *what* God does in the beginning. In John, we see *how* God accomplishes it. As we look at Jesus as someone to believe in, this is foundational. He is not just a good man who walked on the earth and accomplished miracles. This is what sets Christianity apart from cults and other religions. We believe Jesus is God—and has always been God.

His time on earth was a picture of what he has always been and always done—creating all things, speaking life into existence, and upholding the universe. Paul unpacks this further in Colossians, when he says that he is also the "firstborn of all creation,"[2] and that every corner of creation was created by him and for him. He goes on to write, "He is before all things, and by him all things hold together" (Col. 1:17). The believability of Jesus Christ as the Son of God, who has always existed, is not just a nice addition to our belief system—everything hinges on it. Jesus literally walked the earth, even as he literally created all things by his word, and even now is holding all things together. But he doesn't just exist to sit on his throne ruling at a distance. He is a God who draws near.

The Promise to Dwell

If I were to ask you, "Do you think Jesus wants to be with you?" how would you answer? We might think he loves us. We might think he died for us. But do we know he desires to be with us? That is hard to accept, especially if you are in a Christian context where we regularly contrast God's holiness and our sinfulness. Those are true realities that we can't diminish, but not at the exclusion of God being a relational God. I'm a parent of four children. My husband and I love our children and give them consequences when they disobey. But we also love being with them. When we're away from them on a trip, we're excited to return home to them. Dealing with their disobedience doesn't diminish our desire to be with them.

We have a category for parents who don't want to be with their children or who intentionally hold them at arm's length. We call them neglectful. God is our Father. For some, thinking about a father brings up painful memories. Maybe he was distant, abusive, or simply cared more about other things than he did you. These things hurt God's heart because you are created in God's image and deserve to know your value and worth. But it also hurts God's heart because a bad parent tells a false story about what he's like.

After establishing Jesus's eternal existence, John goes on to say in verse 14, "The Word became flesh and dwelt among us," which is universally accepted as "tabernacled among us." For the original readers, they knew what "tabernacled" meant. Or to put it another way, they knew what it meant that Jesus Christ "pitched his tent" among God's people because they had lived for centuries with this imagery in their midst. First, in the garden, God walked among his people—Adam and Eve. He "tabernacled" among them. But sin kept them from his presence, and they were cast out. So God continued to make a way. After God delivers them from Egypt, he gives them instructions for the tabernacle, which is where he manifested his presence among his people. He dwells among his people in the tabernacle (Exodus 25–31). If you read this account in Exodus, you know that in the wilderness, the tabernacle was little more than a tent. God set up camp among his people.

But everyone knew that was not enough. It was what some scholars say, "initial resolution" to this problem.[3] Then God gives them instructions for the temple. This takes all the architecture and detail of the tabernacle and ups the game. God's presence filled the tabernacle and was the place he dwelt among his people. When Solomon builds the temple in 1 Kings 6-8, the dedication of the temple includes God's presence overshadowing everything and filling the temple. It never happened again, not even when Ezra commissions the exiled Israelites to rebuild what had been destroyed by exile. The cry for God to live among them was on their lips, but his presence stayed far off.

God's intent has always been to dwell with this people. And in sending Jesus, his only Son, he makes a way for his presence to live in his broken world among his broken people again. First, he "tabernacles" among us in Jesus Christ. Then he sends the Holy Spirit to indwell all who trust in Christ, calling us, his followers, the temple of the Holy Spirit (1 Cor. 6:19–20).

Scott Duvall and Daniel Hays, two Bible professors and scholars, say that God's relational presence is the centerpiece of the entire Bible.[4] From the beginning of creation until Jesus came through a birth canal and lived in the flesh on earth, God has found a way to "tabernacle" among his people. He is not a God who wants to be far off; he's a God who draws near. D. A. Carson says that the Gospel of John—and particularly these verses in the beginning—ground the entire Bible and the rest of this Gospel. "If this is true," he says, "it changes absolutely everything."[5]

The New Testament unpacks what this promise to dwell means. Up to this point in John, God's people were waiting for the promised Messiah. They had all the pictures and types and foreshadowing, but they didn't have the one they needed. The writer of Hebrews understands this. He writes:

> These serve as a copy and shadow of the heavenly things, as Moses was warned when he was about to complete the tabernacle. For God said, **Be careful that you make everything according to the pattern that was shown to you on the mountain.** But Jesus has now obtained a superior ministry, and to that degree he is the mediator of a better covenant, which has been established on better promises.
>
> For if that first covenant had been faultless, there would have been no occasion for a second one. (Heb. 8:5–7)

The "centerpiece" of Scripture is that God makes a way to dwell among his people again. But he must deal with the incomplete system first. And he does that with his own body. He does that with his very person. God could have been like any other deity in ancient literature and given the task of redemption to a low-level god or kept the sacrificial system going. But he knew that was never going to be enough. We needed *him*.

A lot of words have been written and said from pulpits about John 1:1–18. The wonder that God dwells among us is what anchors these first eighteen verses and the entire rest of the book. I've often thought that this is the point of the prologue in John. But as I've reflected on John's words about Christ, a different emphasis comes to the surface for me. John's main point in the Gospel is belief. My goal for this book is that you read these reflections on Jesus and find him someone to believe in. The incarnation—God coming to earth as a human—is a doctrine we must believe in, that is certain. But the second half of John 20:31 tells us that belief leads to something for us. John is not concerned with giving you facts about Jesus, though they are remarkable. He wants you to be changed by the person these facts point to. It's not enough to know about Jesus. You need to believe that those facts are true, even if they seem entirely unbelievable.

Andreas Köstenberger places the hinge of these verses on John 1:12, which says: "But to all who did receive him, he gave them the right to be children of God, to those who believe in his name." It's not enough to just witness Christ dwelling among us. It needs to change your life—and John says it will in ways you never imagined possible. If you unite yourself to this Christ by grace through faith, you will no longer be far off from God. *You will be his child.*

The incarnation is a wonder, but what John stresses is belief in it. Every aspect of the Gospel of John is driving home belief. And in John 1:10, he tells us that Jesus Christ came to the world he created, but they rejected him. He upholds all things by his word. He spoke all things into existence. The very people he created turned their back on him. His family and blood relatives rejected him. They saw the incarnation with their own eyes, but they didn't believe it. So, John presents a picture of Jesus's time on earth so all who see him face the same question—will you believe? Not just belief in Jesus Christ, but in who Christ reveals. Not just belief that he came, but belief in who he is.

John reminds us that while no one has seen God, those who look on Christ find a direct line to the Father. The incarnation is God's revelation to his broken world, saying, "I'm here. Now you can see me clearly. And if you *believe* what you see, you can be with me again." Up to this point, no one had ever seen God in the flesh. Even Moses viewed him through a veil. In Exodus 34, when God dwells with Moses, he is hidden by a cloud. His presence is there, but Moses can't see him, or he wouldn't make it off the mountain alive. But even Moses is changed by this veiled presence of God (Exod. 34:29). His face is radiant, and the people are afraid to look at him. Now, John writes, someone better than Moses is here (John 1:17). Moses could only give them a veiled picture of God—through the holiness of God revealed in the law. Jesus gives a full picture of God because he's God incarnate and sits at his Father's side (v. 18).

Andreas Köstenberger writes:

> Jesus, who eternally preexisted with God the Father, "has made him known"; he came to give a "full account" of God the Father. . . . In this way, John tells us that we should read the rest of the Gospel as Jesus giving a full account of what God is like and to see both Jesus' works (especially his signs) and his words (his discourses) as a manifestation of God's glory.[6]

Or to put it in a way a child can understand, "Jesus is everything God wanted to say about himself in a person." Köstenberger goes on to say that verse 12 is the "central affirmation in John's prologue."[7] The rest of John tells the story of these beginning verses. We see him as the light shining in the darkness. We see John the Baptist bear witness to him. We see Jesus extend life to all who will receive him. We see some reject him and some believe in him—and not always the ones you expect. We see grace come from his actions, even as truth is coming from his lips. He provides a perfect picture of the Father. Every image before this point—the tabernacle, the priesthood, the kingdom, the temple—was an incomplete picture. But in the Word dwelling among us, we see everything God ever wanted to say and do for his broken world. John calls us to come see this Savior who walks among us and tells us what God is like.

What makes it believable? It almost seems too good to be true, right? I've never seen God in the flesh. And even the ones who did, struggled to believe that he really was God incarnate. In John 14, Phillip asks again for Jesus to show the Father to them (v. 8), and Jesus says:

> "Have I been among you all this time and you do not know me, Philip? The one who has seen me has seen the Father. How can you say, 'Show us the Father'? Don't you believe that I am in the Father and the Father is in me? The words I speak to you I do not speak on my own. The Father who lives in me does his works. Believe me that I am in the Father and the Father is in me. Otherwise, believe because of the works themselves."

It's incomprehensible for even a man who walked alongside Jesus to trust that belief in him is enough. But Jesus gently rebukes him. His actions are enough to explain the Father. His works precede him. Jesus doesn't perform miracles for show. He does it to reveal the Father, the one they've always longed to see but never could come near. Even now, we have what those in the Old Testament, even Moses, couldn't obtain. We see the Father through the works of the Son, in this Word made flesh.

What's even more compelling is in his departure, the works continue. Jesus goes on to tell his disciples in John 14 that in his absence the Holy Spirit will be sent to them (v. 26). The story arc of Scripture is that God has always intended to dwell with this people. And when he leaves to return to his Father, his presence stays. Unlike the "shadows" of his presence in the Old Testament (the tabernacle and the temple), when he comes in the flesh, his presence never leaves them (or us) again.

I was diagnosed with cancer in April 2020, which means I was diagnosed with cancer just as the entire world was shutting down because of a global pandemic. Because it was early during the Covid-19 crisis, hospital protocols required me to do many doctor's visits alone. We traveled to a different city, three hours away, for surgery, biopsies, and scans. As they prepped me for my final scan before surgery, the nurse attempted to calm my fears by saying, "Try to stay calm while this IV drip works." You see, the IV dye the nurse inserted slowly into my veins only did its job if the patient was calm. As it traveled through my body it served as a highlighter for any cancer cells. We all needed this to work. We all needed me to be calm. So, they had me sit in a dark room all alone with the clear instruction: Don't use your cell phone and just close your eyes to relax. *You try telling a young mom who was recently diagnosed with cancer to stay calm,* I thought. But any stress would give an inaccurate read, so I sat in the chair listening to music, trying to will my muscles to relax.

I can't explain it and have never relived it, but I knew God was with me. I've never heard the voice of God audibly, though in that moment, I clearly felt his presence. When my husband couldn't sit with me, or my friends couldn't come see me, I knew without any doubt that God was there. I've carried it with me ever since. He dwells among his people. He did in bodily form in ancient Palestine thousands of years ago, and he does it today through his Holy Spirit. There is no gap in coverage with the presence of the Lord. For all who believe in him, he's with them always.

Perhaps there is no harder time to believe in Jesus than when we are suffering. It's hard to stay near him when everything is stripped from you. It's hard to trust him when your circumstances are untrustworthy. Alongside my own story of finding Jesus believable, you will meet people in this book who have walked hard roads and come out on the other side with stronger faith. They bear the scars of their suffering, but they see Christ more clearly now. They stand as a long line of witnesses who receive him and live. They've been given the right to be children of God—as unbelievable as it may sound to their rational minds. To paraphrase John, the Light shone in their darkness, and the darkness didn't overcome it.

Who Believes?

If John is ultimately hoping for a group of people who genuinely believe in the pre-existent, divine Christ who comes to dwell among his people, how does a person end up in that group? More specifically, *who* ends up in that group?

We will explore ways that Jesus gives life to those who believe in him, but notice verse 13:

> Who were born, not of natural descent, or the will
> of the flesh, or of the will of man, but of God.
> (1:13)

This means that, in a sense, no one can satisfy John's highest hope. There is no family line strong enough to secure your place in God's family. There is no status you possess or financial asset you hold that gives you what you need to get to heaven. You can't buy your way there, and your parents can't pray you out of sin and into righteousness. It's completely outside of your control—and maybe that scares you (or maybe that encourages you).

Indeed, the aim of believing Christ for who he is faces many roadblocks. Some is the impossibility of it all—God becomes man. But some roadblocks are internal. We know our own hearts. We know what we've done. We know what we want to do and are capable of. His light shines in our darkness and we cower.

Except he doesn't shine light to condemn. He shines light to give life (John 1:4). God's people are a rugged group of ruffians who don't know how they ended up there but are glad they did. They are broken by their suffering, sometimes barely hanging on. They are distraught over their sin, often too ashamed to look up at him. They can possess a swagger that is knocked down by repeated embarrassing outbursts of opinion. In short, they are the kind of people who had no shot of believing Christ, or seeing him for who he truly was, or being born into God's family as a child, and yet they did and they saw and they were. *How*, you ask?

Christ extended his hand to open blind eyes. But I'm getting ahead of myself. John 1 is only the beginning.

The Incarnation on Display

The Prologue (vv. 1–18) ends and John hits the ground running, showing us stories of belief and how Jesus is the Christ. At the beginning, the incarnation drives these stories. If you see him as the Word made flesh and believe, you receive the right to be his child (v. 12). This is the burning question for the witnesses in John. *When the God who made everything, and upholds it all right now with his power, walks among you—do you believe?* He doesn't walk among us today, but the question burns as hot as ever. In the Word, we see him. Do we believe?

The rest of John 1 introduces us to many key players in the life of Christ. They explain the Prologue and set the stage for the rest of the book. They come to us in varied stages of belief, and from different circumstances. But all are confronted with the Jesus who draws near, who shows what God is like. We meet John the Baptist, who is confronted by priests, leaders, and fellow Jews about this man he baptized in the Jordan. "Are you the Messiah?" they ask. John had a following in his own right, but he knew his place. He kept pointing to the one who came after him—the one who fulfilled all that had been promised before them.

It sounded crazy that the Messiah walked among them as God incarnate. But how can he be "the Lamb of God, who takes away the sin of the world" (v. 29), if he isn't God in the flesh? The blood of bulls and goats wasn't taking care of it for them. The long and painful history of Israel proved they needed something more potent.

But he doesn't just come as a sacrifice, he comes as a relational person. He comes to "dwell" among his people. He comes to call disciples to himself and walk among them as friends. He comes to call people out of darkness and into light.

When he meets his first disciples at the end of John 1, some follow because of John the Baptist's repeated cry: "Look, the Lamb of God!" (v. 36). They see who he is, but it's a veiled sight. There is an immediacy to their belief, they follow him at once. But as we will see throughout John, it's a process. As the chapter progresses, more disciples join them, but this time they weren't looking for Jesus. Instead, Jesus finds Philip and says, "Follow me." Like any good disciple, he passes it on and finds Nathanael, but is met with skepticism. They've never seen anything good come from Nazareth, surely it can't be where the long-awaited Messiah is from. But Jesus is undeterred by the doubts, which only reenforces both his deity and his believability. He had every right to demand belief from Nathanael, but he doesn't coerce him. He speaks to him the ways Nathanael needs. He needed to see that someone believable could come out of Nazareth, so Jesus reveals his knowledge. He knew Nathanael before Nathanael knew him. And that was enough for Nathanael to hear and believe. He's given the "right" to become a child of God. Nathanael received him.

Finding Belief

The Gospel writers portray a flesh-and-blood Savior. They portray a man who walked the earth. A man who lived a real life and died a real death. They show him rising from the dead and ascending to heaven. They paint a picture of a Savior who weeps, eats, and bleeds. We understand a living Savior. We even understand a dying Savior. But John comes and says, "He has always existed. He even created the entire world." Belief requires us to put our faith and trust in someone—something—outside ourselves. It might not always make sense in our finite minds, but it's true. John urges us to take a hard look at this Savior and find everything he writes worthy of our belief—even if it feels too radical to comprehend.

As I've mentioned before, much ink has been spilled on the incarnation. Entire books have been written about it. Theological arguments have been had about it. But there is something to be said for the effect of the incarnation. There is the "believability" factor that leads to doubt among Christians, that's certain. But there is also the believability factor that leads to life.

No other religion has a God stooping so low. No other religion has a God taking the punishment on himself. No other religion has a God walking among his people and calling them his friends. No other religion has a God who lets people ask him questions, even insulting ones.

But this Christ, he does it all. The remainder of John 1 shows Jesus living out his deity. It's the incarnation on display. At his baptism, John testifies that the Holy Spirit descended on Jesus like a dove—affirming his messiahship (vv. 32–34). John the Baptist repeatedly cries out that this is the Lamb of God, the one promised to remove the sins of God's people. As Jesus continues his ministry journey, he calls his disciples to himself personally. He sees them before they see him. He knows their doubts and stands ready with an answer before they even open their mouths. The incarnation is deeply personal because we have a God who draws near and calls us his friends. He invites them to follow him, and he gives them new names. God could have saved us from a distance, but he drew near. His entire ministry on earth was rooted in relationship because his intent was always to dwell. His rescue plan to resume life among his people is the centerpiece of the Bible—and John 1 is the fulfillment of the story. From the Word creating the world to the Word inhabiting the world, tabernacling among us was always the point. He's that kind of Savior. Of all the world's people to put our trust in, why would we resist believing in such a leader as this?

Philippians 2:6–7 says this about the radical nature of Christ's incarnation:

> who, existing in the form of God,
> did not consider equality with God

as something to be exploited
Instead he emptied himself
by assuming the form of a servant,
taking on the likeness of humanity.

He didn't have to come. He possessed everything he could ever want in heaven. He had to empty himself to assume a human body and tabernacle among us. The God who deserves our service, came to serve. The God who is highly exalted, took up residence in a human body and was born in a barn. He left it all so we could have it all. Is that believable?

A lot makes Christianity seem unbelievable—makes Christ seem unbelievable. As A. J. Swoboda says in his book *A Glorious Dark*, "People would rather follow someone real than someone good. But I think the world will eventually be changed by those who are both good and real."[8]

The God who created the world and everything in it, also left it all to live among the world he made—and bring us back to him. It is as the great hymn writer says, he "emptied himself of all but love."[9] As he walked among the people he created, love compelled him to call them and draw them. He may have emptied himself of the right to exert his deity at all times, but love is who God is and that can never be taken from him. It's what kept him going. Dwelling among his people was always his goal. All we have to do is believe in his name—and that this name is both good and real.

What makes him someone to believe in today—as he is no longer walking the earth? Maybe you are like Philip, and he is calling you to follow him. Do you hear John's words that he is the Lamb of God, and do you believe? Or are you more like Nathanael, looking around at the Christian landscape and thinking nothing good can come out of Christianity anymore? Just as Philip looked at Nathanael, Jesus looks at you and says, "Come and see."

2

He Has Not Been Impressed by Your Religion

(John 3)

WHEN I WAS EIGHT, we moved to Texas from Michigan, leaving behind my mom's family and embarking on a new family journey so my dad could attend seminary. I had never known life outside of church—earning my AWANA badges at an early age and wearing my Cubbie vest proudly.

I still remember my grandma's joy at our decision to move to the "Bible Belt." Hope was on the horizon, founded on the belief that the farther south you went, the more Jesus was acceptable in casual conversation. We were headed to the land of prayer in schools and a church on every corner. Perhaps we could all absorb Christianity because we were around it.

I've lived in the Bible Belt nearly all my life. There is a church on every corner. It is the case that most people you meet claim to be Christian. My high school had a chaplain for our choir, and she prayed before every choir concert. We sang songs written by Christian artists (as long as they weren't "preachy," or you couldn't swap a word out for Jesus). Religion is part of our life in the South, and I imagine in other parts of America too.

But there is a temptation in these regions to think that our proximity to Jesus Christ is enough. Our religious fervor or alignment with the masses who claim his name puts us in the category of "Christian." We equate religion with salvation. Perhaps you've heard these phrases before:

> *I was baptized when I was in high school. Of course, I'm a Christian.*
>
> *I know the books of the Bible, or went to Vacation Bible School, or never missed Sunday school—I'm good with Jesus.*
>
> *I never missed youth group as a kid, but don't attend church much now. I'm not one for Christian gatherings, but I still follow Jesus in my heart, so sure I'm a Christian. It's part of my history.*
>
> *I went to seminary, or I lead a small group, or even am a pastor—I know these things. I'm a Christian.*
>
> *My grandparents started this church. My dad is a deacon in this church. My heritage shows I'm in the kingdom. I'm a Christian.*

The prevailing theme of these comments is something external, right? *I followed the rules, so I'm good. I did all the Bible studies, so I know Jesus. I serve in the food pantry and go on mission trips; it's proof of my salvation.* Even in the Southern Baptist contexts I've inhabited—which would fight to the death for the doctrine of regenerate church membership—claiming your position on the "cradle roll" gets you points somewhere.

If you were born into the church, carried in by your mother weeks after delivery, does that ensure you are safe in the kingdom? If you never strayed from attendance and never wavered in your commitment, are you good? To borrow language from the previous chapter, is your "right" to becoming a child of God dependent on your heritage—or something else?

Some might see a lifetime of service to the church as proof of salvation, or at least religious fervor. Even if someone walks away from the church of their origins in college or young adulthood, we trust they will come back. They prayed a prayer. They walked the aisle at the invitation. They know how to find the verses in sword drills. They can sing the songs from Sunday school. They might show a heritage of faith. But if "they" happens to be you, it also could mean you're missing a key component of what it means to believe in Christ. It could mean you've allowed all these religious rituals to mask a need for something more—better yet, someone more than just the Jesus you pray to when life is hard.

A lot of things threaten to undo our faith in Christ. And many of the things we will look at in this book are hard and sad circumstances that force us to look at him more closely. But there is a sneaky aspect to our lives that also keeps us from believing in him—and that's our religion.

Jesus is someone to believe in when life is crumbling all around us, but he's also someone to believe in when we think we're doing okay. In fact, it's the hardest to believe in him when we think our religion or piety is enough. Self-sufficiency is a sneaky monster. It's central to our fallen nature. Adam and Eve preferred eating their own fruit to the fruit God provided. We prefer drowning in a sea of our own sufficiency to the life-preserver God throws to us through Jesus. We feel the urge to go our own way and convince ourselves that independence is the way to be free. But it's bondage. In the moment, it doesn't feel that way. Until we're drowning, and we know we've made a devastating mistake.

This is where we find Jesus and his new friend, Nicodemus, in John 3. What we find is that it's actually quite common to think you know what it means to follow Jesus—and in true Jesus fashion, he sets the record straight for Nicodemus by exposing his heart.

In the Gospel of John, he uses contrasts to make his point. It's not uncommon for him to situate one character alongside another to show the main idea of Jesus's teaching. Usually in John, it's about the nature of belief. So when we dive into John 3, we shouldn't be surprised to find that John contrasts two very different men. Let's look at the first one.

A Religious Man Can't See in the Dark

In John 3, Jesus encounters a man who thought his title was enough. He was a Pharisee, which we're accustomed to thinking as a negative thing. If someone is too preachy, we call them a Pharisee. If someone expects more from us, or calls us out for our sin—"You're being a Pharisee!" we cry. But in Jesus's day, to be a Pharisee was to be the most religious guy in the room. The Pharisees were respected and trusted leaders in Jewish society. Though Jesus warns his disciples that the Pharisees are hypocritical in *practicing* their own teaching, he still honors the teaching itself, along with the office of Pharisee: "The scribes and the Pharisees are seated in the chair of Moses," he says. "Therefore do whatever they tell you, and observe it. But don't do what they do, because they don't practice what they teach" (Matt. 23:2–3). Why would he say this? Why would he honor their teaching and their office? Because they held the keys to understanding the Law given by Moses. So, when we read that a "man from the Pharisees" comes to Jesus, we should think "an important man is coming to see Jesus."

Nicodemus comes with questions about Jesus and how he's engaged the world around him. But he comes at night, which is an important distinction in John. John often employs contrasts of time to make a point. By coming at night, Nicodemus is breaking rank with his community (the Pharisees and important Jewish men), but not so boldly as to do it during the light of day. But John also uses night as a metaphor for Nicodemus's spiritual condition, which we will see unfold throughout this encounter. Nicodemus has a position to uphold. And he's also still walking in spiritual darkness. The Pharisees and religious leaders don't like Jesus. They don't like his words. They don't like his actions. They don't like his following. But Nicodemus is curious. And perhaps he thinks he can convince Jesus to join their side—to work with them instead of against them. He comes pulling rank and power:

> "We know that you are a teacher who has come from God, for no one could perform these signs you do unless God were with him." (John 3:2)

Essentially, we believe you, Jesus. We know that something important is happening with you. We know God is with you.

But Jesus knows what's in the hearts of people (John 2:24–25). He's not interested in Nicodemus asking questions just to fill his head with knowledge, or go back to his important friends and say he's in "the know." Nicodemus comes to Jesus thinking that his status and religious fervor puts them in the same category. Nicodemus is concerned about the things of God, and Jesus seems to be too, so maybe they have something in common? In his mind, he sees them on similar levels. But Jesus does what Jesus does, and he doesn't answer Nicodemus's statement. He instead introduces a new theme in John—new birth.

I first fell in love with the Gospel of John when I led a group of women through a yearlong study of the book. And I'll never forget one woman's statement when we started talking about John 3 that night in my living room. She remarked that she thought it was kind of funny that Jesus chose birth as his example to a bunch of men who had never given birth. Of course, in a room full of women who had either given birth or experienced a period monthly (reminding them of the possibility of birth), we laughed at her sentiment. Why would Jesus use this example when he's talking to a man?

I think it helps to understand the culture. In Jesus's day, birth didn't happen in a hospital. It happened in a home. Men were not in attendance at the birth, but you couldn't hide from the reality of it if it happened in your own home. Communities were tight-knit. Homes were single-room spaces. If a woman gave birth, everyone knew it—or at least heard it.

While it might be confusing to our modern senses to use the example of birth for a man, Nicodemus understood it immediately. As a religious leader, Nicodemus was acutely aware of the Law's requirements for purification rituals after birth. He knew what birth meant. There is something important about physical birth and spiritual birth that Jesus is trying to connect for Nicodemus. And Nicodemus reveals his heart by his shock at the assertion by Jesus.

> "How can anyone be born when he is old?" Nicodemus asked him. "Can he enter his mother's womb a second time and be born?" (3:4)

This is sheer impossibility for Nicodemus. He thinks he comes to Jesus on a level playing field, and Jesus upends any notion of them being equals. He thinks they're both religious leaders talking "man to man." Jesus shows him he's not even in the same stratosphere. Nicodemus comes with knowledge about God, but Jesus essentially says, "You need more than that to see me. You need something you can't do for yourself." This is why the example of birth is so helpful for him and for us.

While the practice of inducing labor may exist in our current era through the means of modern medical developments and synthetic hormones, we all know that in ancient times, no one could *make* a baby be born. While a woman labored for her child's arrival, no one could know the day or hour that labor would begin or end. You might be able to track cycles to conceive a child, but anyone who has struggled with infertility knows that you can't *will* a baby into existence. And if you've ever waited on labor to start or gone into labor early, you know how much it is out of your control. None of my children have been born anywhere remotely "on time." My twins were born eight weeks early, my second son five days late, and my youngest son four weeks early. For any and every mother, we can know about the process of birth, but we are not in control of it. Even the most "textbook" births are out of our control. Our knowledge about the process doesn't make it happen. Our strategies and best-laid birth plans cannot force our preferences and hopes into existence.

The same is true for salvation, Jesus says to Nicodemus. The Spirit moves where he wishes (v. 8), and we never know the day or the hour of his movement in the life of a person. But to enter the kingdom of God, he must give you new birth. That is a nonnegotiable.

Instead of Jesus answering Nicodemus in the way he's asking, Jesus says, "You actually can't see the kingdom you think you can see, Nicodemus. And the only way to do this is if you get reborn. The only way you do this is by having something happen to you that renews you from the inside out."

And Nicodemus says—that's impossible.

Now we're getting somewhere.

Nicodemus came to Jesus thinking they were of the same ilk. He came thinking he could align himself with Jesus, without having to lose his position. He came thinking that praising Jesus for his signs and powerful phrases would put them on the same team. But Jesus isn't interested in any of it. He wants Nicodemus to see how unattainable any human attempt to enter the kingdom, see the kingdom, or even understand the kingdom is, without a complete re-birth. Without the old Nicodemus dying and the new Nicodemus being born, he will remain blind to the path toward belief.

So, Jesus continues to expose the blindness. In the darkness of night, he gives Nicodemus signs of light, if only he would open his eyes. If only the Spirit would open his eyes.

Nicodemus never comes around to seeing in this text. In fact, Jesus rebukes him for failing to know these things. He tells Nicodemus that, of all people, he should see. He should understand. Why? Because he's a teacher (v. 10). He's a religious leader. He should have knowledge of the Old Testament, the Law, the prophecies, and everything that pointed to Jesus being the Messiah. Here—right in front of him—is the fulfillment of all the Law Nicodemus knows so well. And yet he doesn't recognize it. He comes with unbelief and questions, rather than worship and belief.

Nicodemus is proof positive that knowing the Bible is not enough to open our eyes. Being born into a Christian family is not enough to make us a Christian. Going to a Christian college, or being in ministry, or even attending church won't make anyone believe. Cradle roll can't make you a redeemed child of God. We must be born again. We must walk through the impossible and supernatural process of dying to our old life and being reborn to the new life in Christ.

A Familiar Verse, an Important Point

To prove his point with Nicodemus, Jesus takes him back to the Old Testament. Why? I think it's because Jesus is showing Nicodemus how his knowledge about the Bible wasn't enough. If you want to rebuke the teacher in Israel for his inability to understand that Jesus is the Messiah, take them back to the very words he claims to know by heart. Jesus takes Nicodemus back to Israel's history in the wilderness as an object lesson in the impossibility of being born again without a supernatural event. Everyone knows John 3:16, but we don't often pair it with the verses that come before it. It's worth looking at in its context:

> "Just as Moses lifted up the snake in the wilderness, so the Son of Man must be lifted up, so that everyone who believes in him may have eternal life. For God loved the world in this way: He gave his one and only Son, so that everyone who believes in him will not perish but have eternal life. For God did not send his Son into the world to condemn the world, but to save the world through him. Anyone who believes in him is not condemned, but anyone who does not believe is already condemned, because he has not believed in the name of the one and only Son of God. This is the judgment: The light has come into the world, and people loved darkness rather than the light because their deeds were evil. For everyone who does evil hates the light and avoids it, so that his deeds may not be exposed. But anyone who lives by the truth comes to the light, so that his works may be shown to be accomplished by God." (John 3:14–21)

I think one of the reasons Jesus uses this story from Numbers 21:4–6 is because Nicodemus would have understood it. He's a teacher in Israel, so anything from the Torah was familiar to him. This story comes after God's people have wandered in the desert for a while. After they've seen God deliver them from the Egyptians and so much more, they grumble against him for his provision in the wilderness. It's not enough in their opinion. And God's patience has an expiration date. He sends poisonous snakes in their midst to show them the depth of their rebellion against him. Though many died, God tells Moses to intervene by praying for the people and setting a serpent on a pole. The ones who look to the serpent live. The ones who don't die.

If Nicodemus couldn't understand why new birth was necessary for salvation, or how it was accomplished, perhaps this story from his own history would help drive it home for him. As he does in so many other contexts, Jesus uses the Old Testament stories to show that even back then they were speaking his name and speaking his promises. Salvation didn't change when he came on the scene. It was simply explained in the way he lived and died. He brought it to life. What Jesus is trying to help Nicodemus see is that "seeing the kingdom" was always—past, present, and future—about looking outside of yourself for salvation. It was about (and still is about) the impossible feat of belief in Another for new life—new birth. It didn't matter where they came from, or whose family they were part of, or what title they possessed. They needed something—someone—to stand in their place. They need to *look* and *see* the salvation right in front of them, *believing* God would make good on his promise to save them through the very thing hanging up before their very eyes.

For the Israelites, this was a snake on a pole. For New Testament believers, this is Christ himself—the fulfillment of Numbers 21—who would one day likewise find himself hanging off a beam for Nicodemus. For all of us. The man standing in front of Nicodemus was God's way of making good on his Old Testament promise to save. Nicodemus need only look up and believe it.

When it comes to the snake story in Numbers, R. C. Sproul says that the "implication of this text is that some of those who were bitten looked at the bronze serpent while others did not. Even in their death agonies, in the throes of terror and pain inflicted by these serpents, they would not trust God's prescribed course—even though the cure rate was one hundred percent."[1]

Instead of looking outside of themselves for salvation, the Israelites preferred their own way. They perished for it. In this story in Numbers, salvation couldn't come from themselves. They were desperate and helpless. There was no possibility of salvation for them unless something external delivered them. These were God's chosen people. They had his special hand of protection on them. They saw him descend in a cloud of smoke and fire to guide them. They had the Ten Commandments—words from his very mouth. In short, they had the best heritage and the best code of conduct compared to all other nations. But none of that was enough to save them when their sin reared its ugly head.

This is what Nicodemus needed to see. Your religion won't save you, Nicodemus. Your fervor won't save you, Nicodemus. Your position won't save you, Nicodemus. The only thing that will save you is being changed from the inside out—and that can only happen through the work of Another. All that you have to offer internally won't cut it, Nicodemus. You need to *look* and *see* and *believe* the external saving grace standing right in front of you.

Some spend so much time navel-gazing that they fail to see the salvation available to them. They look at their status, or bank account, or the stack of Christian books on their nightstand, and think they've arrived. Jesus must accept them. We think that too when we equate morality and goodness with new birth. We miss belief because we see our own power as enough. But Jesus says, you must experience the impossible. You must look beyond what's inside you to the One outside of you—to the One who can make all that's inside of you new. You must be born again.

What might this mean for you? It means that whatever you're trusting to help you feel steady—your intellect, your financial health, your good reputation, your gifting, your denominational affiliation, your connection to important leaders, your *being* one of those important leaders, your personality, your high capacity, your moral track record, your ethnic heritage, your eclectic and charming nature, your physique, your political party, your spiritual resume, your meticulous preparedness, your good parenting, your trust in some earthly institution—is eventually going to change, fracture, or crumble beneath you. When you stand before Christ, none of that matters, and it can't hold you up. None of it has an ounce of power against the sin that lies within you and all around you in this world. None of it can make you different or new. When the world gives way in your life, and it will, none of it is something to believe in. You have to look outside of all that to find what can truly save you and hold you steady in this life and the life to come. And when you finally look up and *see* the Savior for who he is, and *believe* him, you'll experience not just the saving power of Christ, but the steadying power of Christ.

The question is: What are you believing in lately? If everything feels shaky to you (and it often does for me), it's time to look up.

A Redeemed Man Gets It

Nicodemus isn't the only story in John 3. John is big on contrasts in his Gospel. Often he starts a chapter with one theme and ends with a contrasting theme. Or he bookends sections with two similar themes to move the book forward. In John 3, the chapter ends with a contrasting response to Jesus that is different than that of Nicodemus.

By this point, everyone is familiar with Jesus's cousin, John the Baptist. While he came on the scene first, Jesus's popularity is gaining on him. And John's disciples are not happy about this.

In verse 26 they come to John saying, "Rabbi, the one you testified about, and who was with you across the Jordan, is baptizing—and everyone is going to him."

Essentially, "We're losing influence here, John." This is no small concern. John's influence was significant. Beyond his miraculous birth, he also had a remarkable ministry. People flocked to him to hear his proclamations about the Christ to come. They came to be baptized and follow in his footsteps. But he had no illusions about what his purpose was on earth. In John 1, as Jesus passes by, John proclaims "Look, the Lamb of God who takes away the sin of the world!" (v. 29). When people ask him if he's the Messiah, he's quick to confess he's not—they should expect another (1:20).

The entire thrust of his ministry was to live out what he says in John 3:30—"He must increase, but I must decrease."

Contrast this response with that of Nicodemus. He comes posturing for power and influence. He comes at night thinking he can align with Jesus. And he comes with a veiled idea about the kingdom of God, thinking that his religious credentials were enough to get him into heaven.[2]

But unlike Nicodemus and John's disciples, John the Baptist gets that this is not tribal Christianity. The only way to new life is through new birth. The only way to cleanse the outside of a person is if the inside is completely made new. The only way to salvation is if the Lamb of God who takes away the sins of the world does just that—gives his life for us. John gets behind that vision and gladly decreases so Jesus can increase. Nicodemus is still confused on why it's not Jesus plus works (or status or family or any other thing we think saves us).

This competition for followers is a struggle for all Christians, from John's disciples until now. In 1 Corinthians 1, Paul rebukes the Corinthian church for their disputes over whom they followed. He writes:

> Now I urge you, brothers and sisters, in the name of our Lord Jesus Christ, that all of you agree in what you say, that there be no divisions among you, and that you be united with the same understanding and the same conviction. For it has been reported to me about you, my brothers and sisters, by members of Chloe's people, that there is rivalry among you. What I am saying is this: One of you says, "I belong to Paul," or "I belong to Apollos," or "I belong to Cephas," or "I belong to Christ." Is Christ divided? Was Paul crucified for you? Or were you baptized in Paul's name? I thank God that I baptized none of you except Crispus and Gaius, so that no one can say you were baptized in my name. I did, in fact, baptize the household of Stephanas; beyond that, I don't recall if I baptized anyone else. For Christ did not send me to baptize, but to preach the gospel—not with eloquent wisdom, so that the cross of Christ will not be emptied of its effect. (vv. 10–17)

This could be written to John the Baptist's disciples too. At the end of the day, there is only one hero. There is only one person we follow. There is only one path to salvation. Our natural fallen tendency is to divide and jump into camps. Nicodemus is in his camp with his religious friends. John the Baptist's disciples place themselves in their own camp with his wilderness zealots. We're in our camps with the Baptists or Presbyterians, or Reformed folks or charismatics—or Republicans or Democrats. We look at the person across the aisle and say, "We're losing followers. Stop them!" Yet, John the Baptist exhorts us that Christ can't be divided. If Christ is being proclaimed, belief is enough. We decrease, so belief in him can increase. Or to use Jesus's words in Luke 9:50, "Whoever is not against you is for you." There's only one team—and we follow our captain.

There's a connection here with Nicodemus and his religious fervor. I've been brought up in a Christian subculture that places a high premium on doctrine, preaching, and knowing the right things about Jesus. I'm thankful for my heritage. I believe much of what I've been steeped in for so long. But like Nicodemus, there's a temptation to assume just because I read the Puritans and prefer hymns to Hillsong that I'm good. I know these things don't save me. (But I sometimes subtly believe that these things influence my standing as a Christian.) If you put me in a camp, I want to be in the *right* one. If you put Nicodemus in a camp, he wanted to be in the *right* one. John the Baptist convicts us all. It's not about camps, credentials, or whether you're a fifth-generation member of your church. It's about being born again into a new family. We must decrease, he must increase.

Nicodemus had to come to the same conclusion as John the Baptist—instead of the right party being something to believe in as our steadiest support in life, the right *person* is. Said another way, the right camp can't steady you or save you over the long-haul, but Christ can. Because Jesus is someone to believe in. He had to see that nothing he did or identified with was enough to give him rebirth. He spent so much time trying to unlock the secret to the kingdom.

But what if there is no secret besides looking on the salvation that comes from another? What if there are no camps except the one where Jesus gathers his people and makes us a family bought by his blood?

As it turns out, when we put our trust in the right "tribe" or "camp," we end up believing in people who eventually, in big ways and small ways, seriously let us down. It's an amazing thing: When

Christ is primary and camp is secondary, we actually get both. We end up not only getting someone to believe in, but a family of diverse people who also believe in him—people we never dreamed we could share a life with. In short, we get Christ *and* the church. That's not to say the church won't also let us down sometimes, or that we won't have valley seasons with other Christians, but because Christ is the One we put our primary belief in, we're steadied and empowered through the rough patches.

The Danger of Religious Credentials

Although many of the other chapters in this book deal with disillusionment because of the harsh realities of life, I included this encounter with Jesus because there is a disillusionment that masquerades as something else. There is a disillusionment that comes not because of a significant trauma or church hurt, but rather a slow slide to apathy. It begins where Nicodemus does.

In their book, *The Great Dechurching*, Jim Davis, Michael Graham, and Ryan P. Burge unpack what they call the "largest and fastest religious shift in the history of our country."[3] We are in the middle of a mass exodus from the local church, the largest in our lifetime. It is estimated that "15 percent of American adults living today (around 40 million people) have effectively stopped going to church, and most of this dechurching has happened in the past twenty-five years."[4] They call this term "dechurching," and you can probably guess why. We are accustomed to having conversations at our evangelism training nights about the "unchurched"—our neighbors and friends who've never darkened a church door before. But the dechurched are the people we once sat next to in youth group. They are the people we took the Lord's Supper beside. They're the moms we served with in nursery and the dads who helped organize recreation games at Vacation Bible School. They know all the religious answers. They probably still have their Bibles. They just don't attend church anymore.

That's a massive amount of people. Even in my own context of the Bible Belt, we are not without casualties. I meet people every week who used to attend church, but now don't. Once back-row Baptists or front-row Pentecostals, they've chosen a different path for a myriad of reasons. When we hear this, we assume it is because of deconstruction, church hurt, the influence of progressive Christianity, or some other factor. But what struck me about Davis, Graham, and Burge's research is that none of those factors were the primary reason people dechurched. In fact, many of the people they found were what they call "casually dechurched," meaning they left the church for no good reason and just never went back. It was a slow slide. As they write in the book, some left without ever intending to stay gone, there was just never a "right" time to return. Some left because life got busy, sports got in the way, or their jobs took too much time.[5] But there wasn't a catalyst moment that led to their departure.

When asked what they believe about God, the authority of the Scriptures, and even obedience to the Bible, many of them still had orthodox views and values. The authors write, "When it comes to our primary doctrines, 68 percent of those we surveyed still believe in the Trinity, 64 percent believe in the divinity of Jesus, 65 percent believe in the resurrection, 62 percent believe that Jesus is the only way to God, and 61 percent believe the Bible is a reliable document for all matters of faith and practice."[6] They go on to write, "While they may have departed from the church, their responses indicate that they may not have departed from the faith."[7] They just didn't care to practice their faith in the church—or anywhere really.

Perhaps at one point, Jesus could have looked at them and said, "Are you a teacher of Israel and don't know these things?" Perhaps at one point they were. These are the former Sunday school teachers, and youth small group leaders. The deacons who gave their life to the church and the women who rocked babies in the nursery. But even that wasn't enough. Like Nicodemus, they needed to look to another for salvation. Like the disciples of John, they needed to decrease so Christ could increase. Since sin entered the world until now, there has only been one way to enter the kingdom—by looking on Another, the Lamb of God who takes away the sin of the world.

But there is also a temptation to believe our good works *after* salvation make us better Christians. We think belonging to a certain tribe makes us "good enough" or our choices about education, working, or even our voting records prove that we're a good Christian. We think if we get our associations right, then our outward appearance as Christians makes us safe. This won't save us from the "casual dechurching" either. If anything, we'll burn out. We will run out our ability to be good enough, left wanting and looking for a better way.

Jesus clears that up for us. He knows what's in all of us, so he's not surprised by our struggles. Instead of condemning us for our failed efforts, he opens his hand to save us. Or rather, he gives his life (as he tells Nicodemus). We can either refuse to look to him for belief and salvation, like the ones who perished in the wilderness. Or we can look to the Son of Man lifted up and find rebirth—plunged into death by our sin, raised to new life through blood.

John the Baptist understood this. He knew that he was not the star of the show. He knew that posturing for power was not the way to the kingdom. He knew that trying to draw a crowd or build an influence was not the way to greatness, death was the only way. He knew that arguing over who is greatest accomplishes nothing because the greatest One was standing right across the Jordan.

Nicodemus would come around eventually. This is not the last time we see him (which I think is such a kindness of the Lord to him). The man who once came at night to Jesus, buries him in broad daylight after Nicodemus's own colleagues send him to the cross (John 19:39). What he didn't see in that moment, he eventually came to see. Believing in your own religious fervor will never be enough. It's like running on a hamster wheel with no end in sight.

But if you want to know the way into the kingdom, look to the impossible way—the way of the Savior. He must increase, we must decrease.

3

He Has Covered Your Past Shame

(John 4)

One of our family's favorite movies is *The Greatest Showman*. It follows P. T. Barnum, the mastermind behind what we now know as Ringling Brothers and Barnum & Bailey Circus. He is a dreamer, always looking for the next adventure, circus act, or way to make a buck. He chases his ambition all the way to a near demise when he gets too close to a female singer in his show. In the aftermath of his realization that his choices are hurting him and his family, the woman scorned sings a song called "Never Enough." It's a crescendo to disappointment and consequences for poor choices, and Barnum wonders if he will recover. He wonders if his family will recover.

He spent his life one step behind his dreams. If he had one hundred people at his show, he wanted two hundred. If he secured a talent that wowed his audience, he wanted to knock their socks off the next night. The life of the circus, and the life of performances, never satisfied. Until he realized he already had what he was looking for. It was standing right in front of him all along. In one of the final scenes of the movie, we find Barnum in a bar alone and broken. He lost his show, his friends, and even his family. His face wears the shame he feels. His past choices have caught up to him and he needs a way of escape.

This is where we find the Samaritan woman in John 4. Her story is a familiar one. It's one of the stories from the life of Christ that we hear frequently, probably because it is so dramatic and beautiful. The Samaritan woman serves as a contrast to Nicodemus in John 4. Jesus tells Nicodemus that his religious credentials can't save him, only Christ can. But here in John 4, Jesus tells the Samaritan woman something completely different. Salvation is still of the Lord, but the way he engages takes on a unique tone.

The story of Jesus and the Samaritan woman is the longest recorded conversation in all the Gospels. And it points to the conclusion John wants the reader to draw in every story he tells—Jesus is someone to believe in.

The Journey to Belief

Nicodemus may not have believed in John 3, but as we saw in the previous chapter, he has repeat interactions with Jesus that eventually lead him to identify with him—perhaps even believe. Belief can be a process. The Bible often speaks of belief in agricultural terms. I do not possess a green thumb, so it can fall flat for me. But if you have ever tried to grow something, unless you buy an existing plant, you are going to be staring at dirt for a long time. The seeds are sown, but they must be watered, fertilized, and nourished by the sun and adequate temperatures. There is no shortcut to sprouting. It takes time and effort that are outside the work of the seed and plant itself. The same is true for belief. It's usually a process. Seeds are planted. Soil is prepared. Plants are watered. Then eventually, when the conditions set in at just the right time, the seed cracks open and newness springs forth.

When we meet the Samaritan woman, the text tells us that Jesus "had" to pass through Samaria (v. 4). Jesus is on a mission to find this woman. There is no reason for Jesus to go through Samaria. We know this because of her response when he asks her for a drink of water in verse 9: "How is it that you, a Jew, ask for a drink from me, a Samaritan woman?" she asked him.

Jews did not associate with Samaritans. This woman knew it, and even later, the disciples acknowledge it (v. 27). It's a scandal to go through Samaria, and an even bigger scandal to talk to a woman in Samaria—let alone a woman with a background like hers. The disdain for Samaria predates Jesus's birth. Israel initially began as one united country. After Solomon's death, his son Rehoboam ascends to the throne and is unable to maintain peace or unity. The kingdom divides, with the northern kingdom becoming Israel (and following Jeroboam as king) and the southern kingdom becoming Judah (and Rehoboam and his descendants as king.) In 722 BC, the northern kingdom is taken into exile by Assyria, but long before that, Israel had given their hearts over to pagan gods. Their capital, Samaria, was a shrine to the gods of the nations, while also maintaining a belief in Yahweh. They even broke rank with Jerusalem and built their own temple. They were judged for their idolatry and carried off into Assyria. Those who stayed behind intermarried with the nations who conquered them, creating "half-breeds." They remained this way until we meet the Samaritan woman, even after their return from exile. The people of Samaria adopted syncretistic practices, were not pure in their lineage, and were considered unclean by the Jews. This is why they had no dealings with Samaritans. They looked down on them and rejected them.

But Jesus, as usual, is undeterred by cultural norms. He values her as a person, created in his image. In talking to her, he shows that he is someone to believe in. He's not boxed in by expectations of his people. He's the Light shining in the darkness, making way for all who believe to become children of God.

After Jesus shows he values her simply by speaking to her, he also disarms her by asking questions. There is a kindness to his inquiry. The woman is shocked that he would not only talk to her, but also ask her for water (vv. 7–9). Instead of answering questions about why he is defying cultural norms to ask for water, he uses the physical need to point to her spiritual need:

> "If you knew the gift of God, and who is saying to you, 'Give me a drink,' you would ask him and he would give you living water." (v. 10)

Jesus tells her he has the water she needs but doesn't know to ask for. Like Nicodemus, she does not understand what he is trying to say, but she's intrigued. Looking at the well in front of her, he says, "Drink from this well, and you will always thirst. The water I give comes from a well that never runs dry" (see vv. 13–14). Who doesn't want that? Who doesn't want to save time in their day by getting water once and never coming back? At least that's what she thinks she needs in the moment. But she's so enthralled by his kindness in offering her living water, the truth he speaks, and the questions he asks, that she is prepared for what comes next. He disarms her so she's ready to see her true need.

His purpose, like with Nicodemus, is to reveal her heart. He's after belief, and he will do everything he can to expose the things that keep us from believing in him. Like with Nicodemus, he uses questions to expose where his beliefs lie. By believing in his religious credentials, Nicodemus walked in darkness, blind to the new life he needed. He found his security in his position and his works, as was conventional for a man like himself. This woman, on the other hand, walked in thirsty, trusting in her experiences to satisfy her and protect her. She found her security in marriage, and when one was over, she ran to the next one in deep hunger for provision and love. Jesus says what she really needs is living water so she will never thirst again. She needs the water from the well of Christ that will spring up to eternal life (v. 14). She needs her thirst quenched so she's kept from looking for security and love in all the conventional places—especially for a woman in that cultural context.

Jesus does all of this before he reveals her life. She needed to see that she was valued by him. She needed to see that he cared about her, because what he exposes is scandalous even for our modern sensibilities. Even in exposing her, he lets her do the talking. In asking her to go call her husband, she reveals that she is currently not married. Jesus responds, "You have correctly said, 'I don't have a husband . . . for you've had five husbands, and the man you now have is not your husband" (v. 17–18). His levels of exposure to her both reveal his care but also reveals his deity. Only God can know these painful details of her life. They've never met before, and even she recognizes how unexpected it is for him to know this about her. In exposing her lifestyle, he also exposes her worship. She might be living an immoral life, engaging in syncretistic religion, but she is also waiting on the Messiah to come (v. 25). Jesus exposes her thirst so he can tell her where satisfaction is found. He holds out the hope of living water because he knows her sinful choices reveal that deep down, she desperately wants to be cleansed, loved, satisfied, and protected. After looking for love and satisfaction elsewhere, she finds her thirst quenched in the place that reveals her deepest shame.

She comes to the well at the hottest point of the day. The text tells us it's noon (v. 6). While we don't fetch our water at the community well, this was a common practice in their culture. But it was not common to go when the sun was at its peak. Even we know all the outdoor work must be completed before it gets too hot. But that's not what she did. She came alone, when women typically came in groups. The well was the community watering hole, where gossip was shared, and partnerships were forged. None of this is available for a woman who has had five husbands and is now living, unmarried, with a new man.

But Jesus comes to her, because he had to pass through Samaria. He had to meet her. In revealing both her past and himself, he saves her and removes her shame.

Unlike Nicodemus, this woman has her life exposed and she "left her water jar, went into town, and told the people, 'Come, see a man who told me everything I ever did. Could this be the Messiah?'" (vv. 28–29).

Why does she believe? Why does she run and tell the town what she's heard and found? I think it's because he told her everything she ever did in terms of external sin and didn't cast her out for it; rather, he solved the *internal* reason she was chasing after security and love to begin with. Her response to his exposure, and his gift, is "can this be the Messiah?" Only a woman free from shame can have her worst sins exposed by someone in authority over her and then run and tell people about it in broad daylight. John uses this contrast between her and Nicodemus to turn the salvation message on its head. The one who should "see" at night because of his religious knowledge, gropes for truth in the dark; the one who has blind eyes in the light has them opened by the one who is the Light. Only a Savior so merciful and gracious can expose her sin yet offer her living water from himself to satisfy. She goes alone to draw water every day because the people who know what she's done don't want to be seen with her. But not Jesus. He knows all things—*he knows her*—and he gets closer. He had to pass through Samaria. He had to save this woman. And then he had to use her to bring others to himself.

I imagine her bursting into town with her testimony took everyone by surprise. They surely knew where she came from, and yet they believe when she shares the good news with them. They run to find Jesus when they hear what he's done. I wonder if part of the reason is because this woman's testimony is not "See how he healed me," but it's "See how he exposed me and he didn't run away." He told her everything she ever did and then said, "I'm the Messiah, the one you've been waiting for."

When Jesus exposes her, she runs to tell others what he's done. In many ways, she's one of the first evangelists. Jesus is undeterred by her past. Her shame and her sin do not keep her from being useful in the kingdom. Instead, it's her greatest asset. She is a living, breathing testimony on the power of this living water! John tells us that her testimony works.

> Many Samaritans from that town believed in him because of what the woman said when she testified, "He told me everything I ever did." So when the Samaritans came to him, they asked him to stay with them, and he stayed there two days. Many more believed because of what he said. And they told the woman, "We no longer believe because of what you said, since we have heard for ourselves and know that this really is the Savior of the world." (vv. 39–42)

Remember what Jews thought about Samaritans? They have no dealings with them. They avoid them at all costs. Generations of idol worship, rebellion, and sin plagued this people. And the Jews kept their distance. But Jesus upends all of it. There is no sin so great, no shame so deep, and no rebellion so long that Jesus Christ can't invade, expose, and remove. He is someone to believe in—from the most religious to the most outcast.

Different Tactics, Different People

Why not tell her what he tells Nicodemus? Nicodemus came at night, not in shame, but in embarrassment. He came with all the reputation, but no shame. She came with all the shame and a shredded reputation. No wonder Jesus uses a different tactic!

When every other woman comes with the crowd to draw water, this woman shrinks back. She's not part of the women of the town who gather around the well for their daily water. She's the one who hides her face until all have gone back home. We all know why people avoid the crowds, especially women who avoid crowds of other women. We don't want to see them. We don't want to engage with them. Sometimes we might even be afraid of them or embarrassed by them. This woman was alone and outcast, so she comes to meet her physical need when no one else will be there. And Jesus knows this about her.

I think Jesus doesn't tell her that she needs to be born again because this would not be news to her. She's had five husbands and is living with a man who isn't her husband. This is a scandal in our modern context, let alone her ancient Middle Eastern context. She carried the shame and stigma of being with at least half a dozen men. Her greatest need is to be made new from the inside out and to be internally satisfied and safe, but she's meeting these needs by running to her culture's typical remedy for security and love for a woman in her position. *Just find another man, another husband. Even if he won't marry you, or even if you've given up on the institution of marriage itself, it's better than being homeless, right?* She has a thirst that can never be quenched, so she keeps drinking from a well that can't stay filled because it was never meant to satisfy. Marriage is a *picture* of Christ and the church, not the real thing. When we make it more than that, we find ourselves forever thirsty, forever craving even more love and security, forever anxious that our stability might be taken away, forever reaching for it all over again if we lose it. Jesus, the true heavenly Bridegroom, comes to pick up the pieces of her shattered picture and give her the real thing.

The shock that this woman feels over her encounter with Jesus is because not only did he engage with her, which was unthinkable to most Jewish men, but he also peered into her soul and exposed her whole life.

Often when we think about being exposed to our core, we feel the urge to hide, like Eve with the fig leaves (Genesis 3). The thought of anyone knowing our deepest sin, our secret struggles, or the things in our past makes us cringe. But Jesus knows what's in all of us (John 2:25). He's not surprised by it, nor is he unable to overcome it.

As I said in chapter 1, I was diagnosed with cancer a few years ago. It came as a tremendous shock because all the normal mechanisms for detecting cervical cancer (like routine pap smears) failed to catch it. If you are familiar with what causes cervical cancer, you know it is caused by a virus, HPV. This is not a virus you catch like you catch the flu or a cold. This is a virus that is only passed through sexual contact. I will never forget where I was when the doctor called me to tell me I had HPV. I felt all the blood drain from my face and scanned my history wondering how and when I got it: *What does this mean for me?* The doctor proceeded to tell me that it was unlikely I had anything to worry about, but we needed to do a small biopsy for a baseline. This would help us detect if any cells changed in the future. She assured me we were in a good spot.

Nothing prepares you for the moment when a doctor says, "You have cancer." I've spent a lot of my life trying to prepare for bad news. This completely blindsided me. On top of the stress of scheduling additional biopsies, blocking off surgery time, and finding childcare. I also had to reckon with the reality that my cancer was preventable. My cancer came from a sexually transmitted disease I likely contracted long before I bowed the knee to Christ. I may have repented and found new life in him, but cancer still grew. A disease still changed my cells. I was forgiven, but I still walked around with the consequences of my sinful choices. For the longest time I didn't want to tell people what kind of cancer I had. People would look at me with pitying eyes and extended sympathy and care—assuming that I was suffering from a cancer that attacked an unwilling victim.

I came to realize that I was living under shame. I wasn't condemned for my sin, because that sin had been paid for by Christ. But I didn't believe that Christ was enough for what I was currently walking through. I didn't think his blood covered this sin that left lingering consequences.

When other cancer survivors wanted to share stories, I made jokes about how my cancer wasn't like their cancer. Breast cancer survivors are attacked from an outside force. Ovarian cancer survivors deserve our sympathy—there are no warning signs. Cervical cancer? We should have just said "no" to our desires.

I hung my head low in cancer survivor circles, never feeling like I fit.

I was afraid to be at the "well" with them because I didn't see us on the same playing field.

In that moment, my story wasn't like the Samaritan woman's because I was looking for satisfaction in the wrong places. But I was like her in that I felt condemned for past choices—and it kept me from accepting what Christ could do and has done for me.

The Samaritan woman kept thinking that if she just found the right amount of living water, she could then have her thirst quenched. I thought if I could just look morally upright and like a "good Christian woman" on the outside, then I would be enough. My past would no longer creep up to condemn me.

Jesus shatters both ideals. Our shame keeps us from coming to him freely and with all our feeble attempts at being filled. He holds out a cup of living water that never runs dry.

A Tale of Two Responses

Jesus takes sin seriously, but he also offers grace freely. He's undeterred by our past—no matter how shameful it is. There is a shame over sin that leads to death and shame over sin that leads to life.

At the end of Jesus's life, he is deserted by every one of his friends. The only ones who stand by him are the women—and John. The ones who promised to be with him to the bitter end, like Peter, cower under the threat of exposure from people as harmless as a servant girl. The ones who walked with him and ate with him daily, like Judas, hand him over to the crowd for a little bit of silver.

Both men denied Christ, but only one found forgiveness. Both men were exposed by the Savior in their choices, but only one lived to tell about it.

Judas ended his life undone by the shame of his choices (Matt. 27:3–5). Instead of finding forgiveness in Christ, he sees no other option but to hang himself. Standing near the Savior only increases his shame, so he does the only thing he thinks will deliver him—takes his own life.

Peter equally felt shame. As he stands around the fire, far enough away from Jesus that he can deny his allegiance, he barely utters the words "I don't know him" three times before he runs away in grief and bitter weeping (Luke 22:62). He knows what he's done. Christ looks him in the face and reveals his soul. One pained look from his Lord tells him "all he ever did."

Jesus is not surprised by our choices. He's grieved by them, but he's not limited by them. Judas was pierced by conviction over his betrayal, but he couldn't turn the corner toward repentance and faith. Unlike the Samaritan woman, who had her sins exposed and believed that Jesus could deal with her sinful past and shameful existence, Judas thought the only way out was escape. In the end it ruined him.

Peter, however, was delivered from the same fate. We find Peter after his denial at the beach of the Sea of Galilee in John 21. Jesus has been resurrected and is fishing with his friends again. You can almost feel Peter's discomfort with being around Jesus. Just a couple chapters earlier, Peter shamefully denied they had ever been friends.

Jesus knows everything we've ever done, and he still welcomes us home. That's what he did for the Samaritan woman, and that is what he does for Peter. He's not afraid of our past, and he's not afraid of what we'll do in the future either.

Just consider his response to Peter here. He tells Peter to feed his sheep. He gives him a purpose, and even repeats it three times to signal restoration (John 21:15–19). He doesn't bring up Peter's past. Peter knows it. Jesus knows it. He simply commissions him to a life of ministry. The Samaritan woman needed the Savior to expose her sinful past so she could see that there is no sin too deep that his grace can't plunge deeper. Peter needs the Savior to forgive him and give him a task in the kingdom so he can see that there is a path toward restoration for even the most shameful of sinners. He needs to be exposed so he can be used by God.

This doesn't mean our sin doesn't have consequences. But where sin abounds, grace abounds even more (Rom. 5:20). He is in the business of redeeming the lost and giving them a story to tell the dying world.

All of this fulfills the purpose verse in John 20:31. Everything written is so we would believe that Jesus is the Christ—and live.

A Promise Fulfilled

Jesus uses the physical imagery to point the Samaritan woman to her spiritual need. She needs her thirsts quenched from a well that never runs dry. She needs her shameful past washed clean by the healing water that Christ provides.

This is not a unique need. It's not the first time the Bible mentions living water. In Jeremiah 2:12–13, God says through the prophet Jeremiah:

> "Be appalled at this, heavens;
> be shocked and utterly desolated!
> This is the LORD's declaration.
>
> For my people have committed a double evil:
> They have abandoned me,
> the fountain of living water,
> and dug cisterns for themselves—
> cracked cisterns that cannot hold water."

For centuries, God warned his people to find their satisfaction in him alone. But the gods of the Canaanites, the idols of their neighbors, and the comforts of the promised land, lulled them into thinking they could trade Yahweh for any other deity. They were wrong—and God held them accountable.

D. A. Carson writes, "They have rejected the fresh, 'running' supply of God and his faithful goodness, choosing instead the stagnant waters of cisterns they themselves prepared, discovering even then that their cisterns were cracked, and leaving them with nothing to sustain life and blessing."[1]

He goes on to write that these same prophets anticipated this moment in John 4. In fact, Isaiah spends a lot of time referencing living water and the quenching of thirst that is provided.

Let's look at a few of them:

You will joyfully draw water
from the springs of salvation,
and on that day you will say,
"Give thanks to the LORD; proclaim his name!
Make his works known among the peoples."
(Isa. 12:3–4)

"For I will pour water on the thirsty land
and streams on the dry ground;
I will pour out my Spirit on your descendants
and my blessing on your offspring." (Isa. 44:3)

"They will not hunger or thirst,
the scorching heat or sun will not strike them;
for their compassionate one will guide them,
and lead them to springs." (Isa. 49:10)

And the chapter in Isaiah that ties it all together is in Isaiah 55:

"Come, everyone who is thirsty,
come to the water;
and you without silver,
come, buy, and eat!
Come, buy wine and milk
without silver and without cost!
Why do you spend silver on what is not food,
and your wages on what does not satisfy?
Listen carefully to me, and eat what is good,
and you will enjoy the choicest of foods.
Pay attention and come to me;
listen, so that you will live.
I will make a permanent covenant with you
on the basis of the faithful kindnesses of David.

> Since I have made him a witness to the peoples,
> a leader and commander for the peoples,
> so you will summon a nation you do not know,
> and nations who do not know you will run to
> you.
> For the LORD your God,
> even the Holy One of Israel,
> has glorified you." (vv. 1–5)

The implication in these verses is that God's people are thirsty. They have a need they can't meet on their own. They have a shame that leaves them exposed. They are looking for someone they can believe in to cover their shame and quench their thirst. For generations, God's people had been looking for love in all the wrong places. The Samaritan woman is a picture of a deeper reality going on all over Israel. God patiently called his people out of their bondage to idols and into a soul satisfying relationship with him—the living water. He dealt with their past shame that kept them from seeing him rightly. He exposed them time and time again. But he also held out his hand to save them. He promised a permanent solution to their repeat rebellion. He would provide living water—he would pour out his Spirit on them, cleansing them from the inside out, and forever satisfying them (John 7:37).

The living water that God provides is not novel in John 4. It's the fulfillment of everything God promised in the Scriptures—a fulfillment that came when Christ walked the earth, exposing thirst and quenching desire by the indwelling, ever-flowing power of his Spirit.

The *ESV Study Bible* says, "To come to Jesus and drink means to believe in him, to enter into a trusting, ongoing personal relationship with him. Both the image of 'coming' to Jesus as one would come to a person and the image of 'drinking' imply not mere intellectual assent but a wholehearted personal involvement and participation."[2] He's always after our belief, but our belief leads to transformation. When we truly believe, we also truly live in obedience to him. We drink from him, the fountain of living water that never runs dry. We tell others about him, like the Samaritan woman. Living water has a transforming effect because it's the very Spirit of the living God poured out on his people.

Our temptation is to find something else—something outside of Christ—to cover our shame and fulfill our longings. We are no different than ancient Israel, this woman in John 4, or Nicodemus for that matter. We know this because the Bible ends with a promise of living water—revealing that humans are the sort who will look for satisfaction and thirst for security until we draw our final breath. In Revelation 7:16–17, the apostle John brings up this theme of living water again—but this time it's at the end of the age:

> "They will no longer hunger;
> they will no longer thirst;
> the sun will no longer strike them,
> nor will any scorching heat.
>
> For the Lamb who is at the center of the throne
> will shepherd them;
> he will guide them to springs of the water of life,
> and God will wipe away every tear from their
> eyes."

When Christ returns to make all things new, then our thirsting and unmet desires will dry up—and we will be satisfied with the living water that Christ provides forever.

When Jesus exposes our sinful desires and attempts at satisfaction, how do we respond? Do we cower like Judas, or come back in repentance like Peter? Do we stay hidden in the darkness like Nicodemus, or do we run and tell like the Samaritan woman in the middle of the day? When Jesus offers us living water, do we see our need and take it? Or do we prefer our broken cisterns—all those things we've believed in to steady us and satisfy us up till now?

The question John holds up is this: What well are you drinking from? Are you drinking from a well that always leaves you wanting more? The well of status, a new car, an upgraded house, designer purses, the love of a man, obedient children, a thriving career, perfect vacations, or even a solid group of friends? Are you steadied by the stuff of Nicodemus—religious credentials and position and law-keeping? Are you steadied by the stuff of the Samaritan woman—strong relationships to protect you or perhaps security and provision in the family pack? None of these good gifts are bad. On their own, they can serve us well. But the message Jesus leaves us with in John 4 is that no matter what happened in our past, or what we're desiring in our present, there is only one well that won't run dry. He is the source of Living Water—he quenches every thirst and has more than enough to go around. When we spend our lives drinking from "broken cisterns" or fail to drink "living water," we easily look for satisfaction elsewhere. The fight for belief begins with drinking the water that always satisfies.

When you find yourself looking for external things to make you happy or to keep you from feeling shame over past sin, Jesus Christ holds out a cup of water and says, "Drink and live."

I was afraid to talk about my cancer story because I believed my past defined me. I may have repented of old sins and found forgiveness, but I failed to believe that in exposing me, Jesus also cleansed me. Romans 8:1 says there is no condemnation for those who are in Christ Jesus. Baptism is a symbol of an internal transformation. We're washed clean by his blood—but also satisfied, indwelt with the Holy Spirit.

Satan wants nothing more than for us to dwell on past sin. He wants us to be exposed only to ourselves, so we live under the condemnation that comes with exposed sin that has yet to be cleansed.

The Samaritan woman got both. Jesus laid her soul bare, but he also provided a way of escape. I said at the beginning of the chapter that the Samaritan woman is meant to serve as a contrast to Nicodemus. Put them side by side and we see similarities in the Savior, but radically different outcomes and responses from them. Andreas Köstenberger summarizes the contrasts in this way:

> What is more, while Nicodemus fades silently into the night, Jesus having reduced him to silence, the woman bears eloquent witness to her fellow Samaritans in broad daylight, inviting them to come meet Jesus and see this remarkable prophet and likely Messiah for themselves. The teacher of Israel is reduced to silence and exposed for his lack of spiritual understanding while the Samaritan woman turns into an evangelist. Quite a contrast![3]

He goes on to say that this continues the "pattern of reversal" we see all throughout the Scriptures. The kingdom of heaven is an upside-down kingdom. The one we expect is not the one who is saved. He writes, "Spiritual receptivity will often be found in those who lack status, power, and prestige in this world."[4]

The ache of the Samaritan woman for security and provision, along with the shame that came with her past, was not a disqualifier. It was the means God used to save her and use her. The same is true for us. Whatever shame over your past sin you may feel, it's not the end of the road for you. It's not a barrier to belief. It's the starting place. If you're living one step behind your dreams trying to make them enough to satisfy you, Jesus sees deep into your soul, but he doesn't cast you out. He welcomes you, satisfies you, saves you, and uses you. His indwelling presence is the living water you're looking for. Will you stop at the well and believe?

4

Living Water Reshapes My Identity

Who Am I If I Can't Get Out of Bed?

As I'm writing, it's almost Olympic season. Like many, my life is consumed with all things Olympics for two weeks every two years. One year, after the Olympics ended, my husband said, "I don't know what to do with myself anymore." We were both sad and a little disoriented because our lives had been immersed in daily consumption of the sports, athlete stories, and national pride that comes with the Olympics.

But our letdown subsided after a few days, and we added the next Olympic cycle to our mental calendar. Something to look forward to.

For the Olympic athlete, it's not that easy. Some face a tight window of competition because of age or injury. One Olympics is all they get. Others devote a lifetime of training, only to compete for a few Olympic games. When it ends, they face what mental health professionals call "post-Olympic depression."[1] Once home in the real world, they must wrestle with the reality of life after competing, or life after losing a dream. They contend with feelings of melancholy, even with a handful of gold medals. Many have spent more time training than any other milestone in their life. Their identity is wrapped up in their sport, and when it's over they wonder who they are.

All of us are susceptible to this, though on a smaller scale. We aren't Olympic athletes (at least I'm not), but we've all wondered who we are at some point. Up to this point, we've looked back at Jesus Christ from the angle of our past. We've seen his existence from the beginning in John 1. He's challenged our belief in our own religious fervor in John 3. And he's shown us how our past isn't a barrier to belief in John 4. He's the one who satisfies every longing.

But as we wrap up this first section (and as we wrap up every section), I want to show you real people who have found Jesus to be someone to believe in—even when wrestling with a shift in identity.

Post-Olympic depression, and any depression after a dream ends, is real. Even the most faithful Christians wrestle with disorientation when what they expected is not what they experience. We know our identity is secure in Christ, but sometimes we feel the exact opposite. We need to see we aren't alone in that.

Katie's Story

In late spring of 2022, Katie began experiencing episodes of tachycardia (high heart rate) for no reason. Initially, she was diagnosed with something else, but her heart consistently ran high, leaving her depleted of all energy. She had young children, but was completely housebound and bedridden, with no relief in sight. By August, she was diagnosed with POTS (Postural Orthostatic Tachycardia Syndrome), but because there were no specialists in her area, finding relief and treatment made her symptoms continue. The worst symptom was a debilitating brain fog.

"I couldn't concentrate, I was forgetful, I couldn't think clearly which left me unable to read my Bible, pray, or even comfort myself with what I knew to be true about God," she said to me in a phone conversation.

Perhaps you can relate to Katie's joy in studying Scripture. Prior to her rare illness, she enjoyed a life of studying, teaching, and writing about the Bible. She even sensed a call to ministry. She said, "When I became sick, I was not only worried that I'd lost my calling but that I would lose the closeness with God I had once enjoyed. How could I enjoy the peace, contentment, strength and wisdom that comes from beholding God in his Word if I couldn't read or pray anything other than, 'Please help me'? I feared that if the strength of my faith was measured by my Bible reading and prayer life, then I must be faithless."

Her time in her bed led to fear of missing out and missed opportunities. And sadly, there were opportunities she missed—even one she had spent her adult life longing for. This only increased her disorientation that she was losing herself with no end date in sight.

Even after receiving a diagnosis, the months leading up to it left her depleted. Because of her rapid heart rate, she felt like she'd run a marathon every day. Her body worked overtime to compensate, which only exacerbated her brain fog. The thing Katie loved most—the thing she sensed God made her for—was nearly impossible at the level it was before. It forced her to reckon with her identity, but also her heart motivations in ministry. It's a hard tension for the believer. We say that if you are abiding in Christ, you will bear fruit. We say that we are supposed to work out our faith with fear and trembling. But what if there is no outward visible sign of working toward growth? If prayer and Bible reading are absent, where is your faith? This was her struggle. She questioned if her faith was even real when she couldn't do any of that.

> Before I got sick, I loved working for the Lord. Loving the work more than I was loving him. Brushing that conviction aside, I had this moment praying, "Lord, you may take things from me to humble me, but please don't take my mind." I love thinking about the things of God, reading, studying, writing. It's not funny, but I specifically prayed for it and God took that from me. It was identity-shaping for me. *Where do you find your worth and identity when God takes your work?* He literally took my ability to think for long periods of time. I didn't even know cognitive dysfunction was a thing, but that's what God took.

The season of brain fog gave her new perspective, reminding her that her identity is in him. Her worth is not in what she writes, or how well she teaches the Bible, or even in her daily quiet time. Her worth and identity are in him alone. Coming to this realization, even when her brain fog isn't fully healed, has led to a new humility in her. God has slowly given her back some cognitive function, and for that she is grateful. It's helped her hold her dreams loosely, even as she still loves studying, writing, and teaching. She said, "I don't want to do it if God doesn't want me to. If God doesn't want me to publish a book or write, I'm happy to do what God wants. Not what I want. I only want what he has ordained for me. I don't want to chase the prestige that comes with the work. And I know I had been chasing it before."

God met Katie in that long season of cognitive dysfunction. She couldn't study like she had before, but he provided for her in other ways:

> My trust in God grew as God slowly and gently met me where I was in that season. I could give

God whatever mental capacity I had that day (which was usually very small), and he would bless it for my good. I thought often of the poor widow in Mark 12. She brings her offering to the temple. Jesus is there and she gives two coins that equal a penny, and he praises her for giving everything. I clung to that. There were days when I felt like, mentally speaking, all I had to give were two coins—less than a penny. As far as giving my times and thoughts to God, all I could cry out was "please help me." God blesses those small offerings and uses them and can make it fruitful, even when it seems not enough.

I couldn't read Scripture in the way I had done before, and this made me question my faith. But I discovered that I could listen to it being sung, so I would listen to *The Corner Room* sing the psalms on repeat. Two psalms stood out to me, Psalm 16 and Psalm 23. These are songs of confidence, and that is what I needed. I had lost my confidence, not that he wouldn't keep me, but that I had lost my calling or ability to think and speak and to talk to other people about Jesus. I needed that confidence that I still had value and my identity wasn't lost.

I couldn't pray, but I could ask others to pray on my behalf. And when I finally started to feel better, I discovered a strengthened faith and renewed hunger for his Word that could only have come from God's constant care and faithfulness to me. It was then that I found him most worthy of my trust.

God didn't waste all her years of faithful study. She couldn't read, but he would bring Scriptures to mind for her. In particular, 2 Corinthians 4, reminding her that she had the treasure in a jar of clay, even when the clay was cracking. She was suffering, but not abandoned.

In the months after, she spent time in the book of Job and the Gospel of John. In both books, she found that Job and the disciples are wrestling with similar questions through the lens of their own suffering and circumstances. Is God believable? Is he trustworthy? Like Job, her circumstances didn't match with what she knew about God. In the months and years after the onslaught of suffering, she identified with the long line of believers in Scripture who brought their complaints to God. And she's been comforted. "God can work with our complaints," she said.

A Renewed Identity

Katie still suffers from POTS, though not to the degree that she did in the beginning. She calls herself "better, but not healed." The cognitive dysfunction is gone, and she can concentrate. She has even started teaching Bible studies again. But there is no cure for POTS, so she will always be in management mode for her disease. It's a battle she will fight for the rest of her life.

But there is something more important, something spiritual, that is healed in her—she has a redefined identity. When she first got sick, she thought she was losing her faith. Instead, God used her suffering to *grow* her faith. She is less afraid, insecure, and inhibited than before. Like the psalmist, she can say, "It was good for me to be afflicted so that I could learn your statutes" (Ps. 119:71).

This spiritual healing didn't come without tremendous pain and wrestling through her losses.

> As I began to heal and recover my cognitive capacity, I discovered the most remarkable thing: My faith was not only sustained but had actually grown during my illness. I saw firsthand that the strength of my faith was not dependent on how tightly I was holding on to my spiritual disciplines, but on how tightly Christ was holding on to me. My faith held fast because he is strong. All of this gave me a greater awareness of my utter dependence on God to sustain me in weakness, even when that weakness made it difficult to draw and feel close to him.
>
> The hardest thing was to trust that Jesus would care for, sustain, and see me through my sickness when I was incapable of seeking his face through Bible reading and prayer. It exposed an underlying belief of works-righteousness that I didn't know was there. I believed that Jesus needed my help to hold my faith fast. It was hard to trust that God could use the kind of cognitive dysfunction that prohibits Bible study and sustained prayer for my good.

She recalls a moment after the brain fog, when she visited with a friend. As they met to talk and pray, the words Katie spoke took her by surprise. She said, "They were absent of the anxiety and fear and inhibitions that I had with praying out loud. God has grown my faith through this. The only reason I could see that this was happening is that he had used suffering to rid me of things holding me back. I've seen it so many times since then, in conversations, in writing, and in my prayer life. It's all more fervent, scriptural, and real. I haven't fully figured out how it happened, but God grew me in my suffering without me realizing it."

When asked why she continues to trust Jesus now, she said he's proven himself to be trustworthy to her. How can she not trust him still?

> When I had nothing to offer or give, he was holding me fast and providing abundantly for me. I saw his trustworthiness through the people in my church in the way they cared for me, providing for my physical and emotional needs. I saw his trustworthiness, down to the doctors and therapists at the right time. They provided God's care when I needed it most. Now that I'm back reading his Word, it's richer. My faith is stronger having gone through suffering. I've now seen people in the Bible who were weak and not strong by the world's standards and seen how God used them. I keep coming back to who he has revealed himself to be in his Word. His Word and my experience reveal he is trustworthy.

When we first meet a person, one of the first questions we ask (apart from their name) is "What do you do?" This question feels natural to ask because according to the values of our present culture, a person's output—their productivity and contribution to the world—is their (and our) primary badge of honor. Whether we flaunt this badge in conversation or in a perfectly curated social media profile, we're projecting a persona and an image into the world all the same. It can look a lot of ways, depending on the domain of our work, but it all serves to reinforce our self-perceived identity:

Look at this three-course meal I just made for my family.

Remember: I'm a cook.

Look at this Bible study I just finished.

Remember: I'm a Bible scholar.

Look at this classroom I just spoke to.

Remember: I'm a teacher.

Look at this 12-hour shift I just completed at the hospital.

Remember: I'm a nurse.

Look at this non-toxic makeup I'm wearing as I knead this all-organic bread dough.

Remember: I'm a health enthusiast.

Look at this conference room I just impressed with my fancy spreadsheet presentation.

Remember: I'm an accountant.

Look at this massive book I just finished reading, along with the 40-page paper I wrote on it.

Remember: I'm a student.

Look at this huge event I just single-handedly pulled off for my church.

Remember: I'm in ministry.

> *Look at this awesome parenting decision I just made for my impeccably dressed six-year-old.*
>
> *Remember: I'm a mom.*
>
> *Look at this VIP client I just landed over dinner at this incredible gourmet restaurant!*
>
> *Remember: I'm a businessperson.*

Given the constant energy it requires to present such images to the world around us, it's no wonder that we are completely disoriented when we lose our work, our dream, or even the thing we do most (like a sport, a career, or even motherhood). Our natural inclination is to define ourselves by our ambitions. For the believer, it's a near constant battle to redefine our identity around the one who created us and redeemed us. And it's even harder when we find our identity in something that is adjacent to him, or even serves him, but isn't *in* him, as it is with Katie's story. The beauty of Jesus is that he is undeterred by our mistaken identities. He lovingly calls us back to him, sometimes through painful circumstances. But we can never lose him—because he can't lose us.

Katie walked through a deep valley and is still emerging from it. She may have lost her ability to teach, study, and write for a season, but she never lost her true identity, which is in the God who came to dwell among us, causes us to be born again, and satisfies our every longing. She said,

> Our vision, what we can see, and reality are all so limited. Sometimes we look at our circumstances and think God can't work with this. We're too weak, too limited, or too incapacitated. We say, "I can't see how God can use it for good." But when Jesus promises to hold us fast, we can believe

> him. Our circumstances are not too big for him. He really does bless us through the suffering and works the things for our good. It seems almost miraculous, by the world's standards. It's impossible for anything good to come from being as incapacitated as I was. But what we see is not always what is true.

Jesus reshapes and relocates our identity. He is committed to us. And what he accomplished in the past, secures our future. He's someone to believe in.

PART 2

THE SAME IN THE PRESENT

5

He Is Not Disappointing You

(John 9–10)

In my twenties, I was part of a church plant sent from a large church. We set out with excitement and vision for a new thing in a new neighborhood in a diverse city. Within a couple of years of planting, the pastor was asked to resign over a relationship with a woman who was not his wife.

As a young, single woman, I joined the church plant with earnestness and energy. But I had never heard of this type of situation happening before. Neither had my friends who came with me to help plant, carrying with them the same innocence. We left our thriving multi-site megachurch to start this new movement. But we, fresh-faced twenty-somethings, got a stiff dose of reality on a cold autumn night. All the dreams we had for the church were dashed in one members' meeting.

The fallout was devastating. Some people left the church in support of the ousted pastor. Some people stayed, trying to make it work with the interim pastor. Some people floundered, wondering if the local church was the place for them anymore. *If pastors can't be trusted, can Jesus?*

It's been almost two decades, but the ramifications of that shepherd's fall still echo through the lives of the sheep. Relationships that never recovered. Families that fell apart. Faith journeys that ended abruptly. A neighborhood was left without a healthy church as its center. I wish I could say others in the church only faced this once. But I've lived long enough and seen too much.

There are disappointments that have the potential to change our trajectory. There are setbacks where the bounce back is delayed, or never happens. In the wrestling match of life, getting up from the mat is harder with these crushing blows.

When a marriage crumbles.

When a trusted leader deceives us or hurts us.

When we lose status or influence because of our faith.

When we find ourselves alone because of our convictions or because of conflict.

There are disappointments that threaten our faith largely because they aren't ours alone to bear. It's one thing to be confused and frustrated because of something that happens only to us, but when other people are involved (like family members or an entire church), it's hard to find our way forward.

In recent years, there have been a myriad of pastoral failings that have plagued churches, missions, and ministries. Perhaps it's more frequent now, but my guess is that Christian leaders have always been disappointing Christ's sheep. We just have more access to the carnage in this digital age.

Today, we see people fall in our own communities, but also in the church across the country. We hear of moral failings or marriage struggles in our neighborhood, but also amidst the people on social media. While we share the wealth of wisdom in responding to such letdowns, we also share the burden of knowledge. We can't "unknow" what we know—so we ask: "Does this mean all hope is lost?"

The challenge before us is to disentangle our experiences of disappointment with what we know about Christ. And when those experiences are part of our faith communities, churches, or even our favorite Christian celebrities, disentangling requires care and time.

There are disappointments in leaders or people that exist because of their fallenness or perhaps simply because of their limitations. A pastor fails to follow up on getting coffee with us, and that hurts our feelings. A professor is too busy to meet or listen to our concerns. A counselor misunderstands our struggle and gives advice that makes it worse. A spouse can't meet all our needs, so we pull away. A parent doesn't share our joy in a new opportunity, so we feel brushed aside. These are hurtful, but not outside the realm of recovery.

But there is a neglect that cuts even deeper. When ministry leaders abandon us or sin against us, our faith in God is tested. It's hard to know where our trust in leaders ends and trust in God begins. Ministry leaders hold a level of authority and influence in our lives, so when they disappoint us it's hard not to see their behavior as a stand-in for God's.

Where do you go when the *people* you're supposed to trust for spiritual health are the culprits of the opposite in your life? Where do you go when the *place* you're supposed to find guidance is the space you face the most hurt? John 9–10 gives us a template and clarity.

Context (Crux) of Suffering

In John 9, Jesus encounters a man born blind.

As Jesus walks along the road, the man stands out. His suffering was so severe that it leads Christ's disciples to ask Jesus if it was the man's sin or the sin of his parents that made him this way (John 9:1–2). This was a common assumption in this time period, and if we're honest, a common notion today. We see someone suffering and wonder if he caused it himself. We see someone living under the weight of this broken world, and in the back of our minds doubt emerges. *Could she have prevented this?*

This sort of speculation is what this man lived under. Up until his encounter with Jesus, he spent his whole life with this weight of suspicion on him. *Is he the reason he is blind? Are his parents the cause of his blindness?* That kind of gossip can undo a person—always walking around wondering what people think about your condition.

But Jesus doesn't let the conversation go there. He tells his disciples that it wasn't anyone's sin that led to this man's blindness. This man's condition was so Jesus could come and heal him—showing the works of God to all who could see (9:2–3).

In John's Gospel, as we have already seen, these signs are incredibly important. This is the sixth of seven signs. Each sign drives home the reality of Jesus's identity. John is deeply concerned we see Jesus rightly. The signs reinforce the key idea that Jesus is not only the Christ but God himself in the flesh, and all these signs are intended to lead to belief. He's not just a miracle worker—as God, he demands our trust and worship.

And in this sixth sign of the Gospel of John, Jesus shows glory yet again. Jesus spits on the ground, makes mud with the saliva, rubs the man's eyes with the mud, and then tells the man to go wash off in the pool of Siloam (which means "sent"). The man does as he's told, and when he returns from the pool, he is healed of his lifelong blindness (9:6–8).

In any healing story, the miracle should be a cause of rejoicing. A man born blind now sees! But like every other instance of Jesus displaying his power, the rest of John 9 shows us that the religious leaders are indignant. The people, who knew the man his entire life, are confused. Rather than marveling at this act of mercy to a suffering man, they question the validity of the entire encounter. They bring the newly seeing man to the Pharisees to check him. To make matters worse, this healing happens on the Sabbath. Like other instances of healing, Jesus releases this man from bondage on a day that the Pharisees expressly forbid any work, even if it means mercy to the one suffering.

And where is Jesus in all of this? Nowhere to be found.

You would expect him to be right there, wouldn't you? If he wants "the works of God" to be displayed in this man's life, wouldn't the one who worked wonders be in the vicinity? Instead, the man endures a full-blown interrogation from neighbors, friends, and religious leaders by himself. And no one believes him. To add insult to healing, his own parents keep him at a distance. They are the only ones who can really vindicate him in this moment. His mother gave birth to him. His father experienced his inability to see. His parents likely cared for him until he became a burden to them and resorted to begging on the side of the road. Yet when his own parents are asked by the Jews how the man is healed, they defer to him, rather than defend him. Fearing the Jewish leaders, his parents state the facts, but make no claims about Jesus.

A second time, the Pharisees bring this newly-seeing man forward. But he can only speak to what he knows—"I was blind, and now I can see!" And all they can do is speak to what they fail to know—they are blind, and only grow more blind.

After all of this, he is cast out of the presence of the religious leaders and his friends and family. Worse than that, he is blamed for his original blindness on his way out (9:34). He starts the story blind, and though he can now see, he ends the story a greater outcast than when he began.

Jesus is still nowhere to be found.

Jesus heals the man, and then quietly slips away while the man is interrogated by everyone he's ever known. (When John 9:35 reintroduces Jesus in the story, we notice that he learns of what this newly healed man had to endure not by witnessing it himself, but by hearing about it through the grapevine. Somewhere between the man's journey to the pool and back, Jesus made his way elsewhere.) By all accounts, this man seems left to himself to face the accusers. What good is it to be healed if Jesus leaves you when you need him most? What good is it to see clearly if everyone you've ever loved won't share in your sight now? Or doesn't want you in *their* sight?

This is what this man faces. His parents won't stand beside him. His friends and neighbors relentlessly question him. And the religious leaders he's supposed to be able to trust just lumped him into a group of disciples who fail to keep the religious law. Instead of being welcomed into the temple, healed of any suspicion of wrongdoing, he's shown the exit. Even his opportunity for worship and cleansing is removed by being cast out.

The man was disappointed in every relationship he once held close. He was healed of his blindness. But he traded one ostracism for another. Was Jesus worth it?

This is where we land sometimes, isn't it? You're committed to Christ, but your friends reject you. You're walking with Jesus, but your parents don't understand what happened to you. You're committed to the local church, but church is hard and pastors or even fellow church members can disappoint you. You're healed by Jesus, but the most religious people among you fail to stand beside you.

What good is it to be healed by Jesus if you lose everything and everyone in the process? Where do you turn when the shepherd you think you can trust casts you aside?

The Good Shepherd Shows Up

This man's healing is the backdrop for one of Jesus's most famous "I Am" statements. In addition to the seven signs in John's Gospel, Jesus also uses seven "I Am" statements about his identity. These statements reinforce spiritual truths. What's striking about them is that Jesus always gives them in the context of a conversation. He doesn't reveal himself on an island or in a vacuum. He does it in relationship—for the people he came to save.

Consider the context of Jesus saying he is the Good Shepherd in John 10. This blind man who now sees is cast out by the religious shepherds of his day. He's lost trust with his parents. He's cross-examined by the only neighbors he's ever known. And Jesus finds him (John 9:35). His entire reason for healing this man is not so he could see with his eyes, but so he could see with his heart. In seeing Jesus with his eyes, he comes to understand who he is—the Son of Man, the one who comes to seek and save the lost.

Again, this is the backdrop for Jesus's multi-layered statements on his shepherding.

In the aftermath of his suffering, this man (and all who are listening) needs to see Jesus on full display. He needs to see his salvation story in color. Jesus is the one who calls the sheep by name (John 10:3). He is the one serving as the doorway to their salvation, protection, and life (10:7–10). He is the one who lays his life down for the sheep (v. 11). He is the one who knows his sheep intimately (v. 14).

He is the Good Shepherd. And as he makes this statement in the hearing of the man born blind, he confronts the bad shepherds (the Pharisees) by placing himself in stark contrast to them. It's subtle, but it's indicting. He declares himself the Good Shepherd to the very shepherds who fail the sheep.

> Other shepherds might abandon you when it gets hard or dangerous, but not the Good Shepherd.
>
> Other shepherds might come to steal, kill, and destroy, but not the Good Shepherd.
>
> Other shepherds might cast you out because you're a threat, but not the Good Shepherd.
>
> Other shepherds might be afraid of what your new life might do to their pasture, but not the Good Shepherd.

The Good Shepherd does not disown you.

The Good Shepherd only comes to give life. The Good Shepherd only comes to heal. The Good Shepherd does not come to take; he comes to give.

Every generation needs this reminder. Every generation is plagued by bad shepherds. Every generation faces a crisis of faith in leadership, institutions, and even shepherds—those who would rather cover up sin in the name of Christ instead of exposing it and would rather preserve the establishment than lay down their lives for the sheep.

Such shepherds truly are dangerous, and their harm to the sheep is deeply damaging. But the worst kind of danger is twofold: one, assuming we're the first to deal with such a problem at such a shocking level—as if no one else has ever experienced such betrayal and spiritual trauma to the degree we have. Or on the flipside, the second danger is this: thinking we have somehow grown past such crises in our modern era—as if we're the generation that finally arrived to the point in history where Satan has retired from his schemes and sin no longer exists, grows, or corrupts the human heart.

Now, I'm not saying that shepherds shouldn't be held accountable simply because their behavior is common to history. Nor am I saying that their sin should not be exposed or mourned—as if looking the other way or blanketing over the issue could ever heal it. What I *am* saying is this: we will deal with faults and failures in leaders (and in ourselves) until Jesus returns to make all things right. I am saying that too often, in our attempts to simply *honor* our leaders as they *mimic* the Good Shepherd, we are sometimes tempted to *equate* earthly shepherds with the Good Shepherd himself. And I'm saying we're not the first to do that by a long shot.

An Age-Old Problem

Ancient Israel had this problem too. In Ezekiel 34:1–4 (ESV), Israel had some bad shepherds. God sent Ezekiel to confront these religious leaders who had failed to guide and lead God's people rightly. He writes:

> The word of the LORD came to me: "Son of man, prophesy against the shepherds of Israel; prophesy, and say to them, even to the shepherds, Thus says the Lord GOD: Ah, shepherds of Israel who have been feeding yourselves! Should not shepherds feed the sheep? You eat the fat, you clothe yourselves with the wool, you slaughter the fat ones, but you do not feed the sheep. The weak you have not strengthened, the sick you have not healed, the injured you have not bound up, the strayed you have not brought back, the lost you have not sought, and with force and harshness you have ruled them."

Ezekiel goes on to explain what happens to the sheep in light of this laundry list of bad behavior. The shepherds have failed them over many generations. They are scattered and devoured. They are left to fend for themselves, devoid of any leadership. They are homeless and aimless. And yet, Ezekiel says, they are not without hope. The shepherds are not at the top of the leadership chain. There is someone above them. God is the chief shepherd, and he says through Ezekiel that these shepherds will face their judgment. All the sheep who are wandering aimless, left to waste away by the bad shepherds, will be called home by the Good Shepherd. Indeed—God promises that he will, *himself*, come to them as their Shepherd one day, revealing what a true leader was always supposed to look like:

> "For thus says the Lord God: Behold, I, I myself will search for my sheep and will seek them out. As a shepherd seeks out his flock when he is among his sheep that have been scattered, so will I seek out my sheep, and I will rescue them from all places where they have been scattered on a day of clouds and thick darkness. And I will bring them out from the peoples and gather them from the countries. . . . And I will feed them . . . with good pasture. . . . I myself will be the shepherd of my sheep, and I myself will make them lie down, declares the Lord God. I will seek the lost, and I will bring back the strayed, and I will bind up the injured, and I will strengthen the weak, and the fat and the strong I will destroy. I will feed them in justice. . . . And you are my sheep, human sheep of my pasture, and I am your God, declares the Lord God." (Ezek. 34:11–16, 31 ESV)

For folks who know their Old Testament pretty well, which Jesus's hearers did in John 10, Jesus knows exactly what he's doing when those famous words ring out: "*I* am the Good Shepherd." He's claiming to fulfill the promise God made all the way back in Ezekiel's' time, which means he's claiming to be the Lord God himself. And think of his general audience: Jews not only under Roman occupation, but under the weight and rigidity and cruelty of the Pharisees too. In other words, his general audience are those who are currently under terrible leaders. Moreover, consider his immediate audience: a newly healed man who had just gotten cast out of the Pharisees presence for simply being able to see. Talk about a generation of shepherds who used their power to hurt the sheep!

"I am the Good Shepherd." Those words certainly triggered something in their minds. Surely it reminded them of Ezekiel's words about good and bad shepherds. Standing before them was a visual representation of the good and the bad. A man healed by the Good Shepherd and the bad ones who reject his testimony on a technicality.

Hear this: Jesus has no tolerance for bad shepherds. He didn't in Israel's day. He didn't when he walked on this earth. And he doesn't today.

R. C. Sproul says:

> When God looked at the corruption of His people, He laid the responsibility at the feet of the priests and the clergy, who had been charged by God to feed the flock. . . . The leaders of Israel failed to shepherd the flock. The Pharisees failed to shepherd the flock. Like them, the leaders of the church are called to be shepherds, but we too often fail to shepherd the people of God.[1]

Who Do You Trust?

When we see bad shepherds, there is a temptation to reject good ones. We all know of people who once walked with Jesus or served in our churches, only to walk away or deconstruct after a painful encounter with a leader. Some of these stories are public for all the world to see, but many others are quiet and lesser known, though equally devastating. It's a weighty thing to be entrusted with people's souls. Leadership failures have consequences, often more far reaching than we realize.

The story of the man born blind is a cautionary tale for any leader who holds authority over people's spiritual well-being. There is an expectation on leaders to not repeat the mistakes of those who have gone before us.

Jesus has harsh words for the bad shepherds, but he's far more concerned that we believe on him than that we reject all the bad shepherds out there. He wants us to see him and in seeing him, we see everyone else rightly. He will deal with the bad shepherds. But it should also comfort us, because we aren't the ones who have to see justice meted out. The Good Shepherd takes care of his sheep—and keeps all other troublemakers out. He has strong words for the bad shepherds, but he's the one who deals with them. Not us.

This can be a tender subject for a lot of people, myself included. Disappointment and abandonment from spiritual leaders are sorrows that lead people to reject Christ altogether. It can be hard to disentangle the Good Shepherd from the bad one. It can be hard to distinguish the safe sheep pen from the one that caused you so much pain.

This is why John addresses the situation. It's why John 9 and 10 go together. The man who was rejected by the earthly leaders—as well as the friends he held dear—saw that Jesus is the one who did not reject him. He saw it in contrast to all the shepherds in his rearview. He wasn't oriented rightly until he was given sight. He couldn't see the Good Shepherd until he walked past the bad ones.

Sometimes we need these resets as well. We can't disentangle from our past experiences until our eyes are opened and we are face to face with the Good Shepherd. In the wake of such pain, it is helpful to ask ourselves questions: *Where do I need a re-orientation? Where do I need to reassess my expectation of leaders, relationships, and the church?*

In the words of Russell Moore, "Where do I idolize the institution and where do I idealize the institution?"[2] Both lead to disappointment when we fail to put them in their proper perspective.

As we consider our experiences with shepherds, leaders, and institutions, we should show proper honor, where it is due, while also holding to realistic expectations. If we trust the Good Shepherd, he protects us from idolatry and idealizing. There is room for failure, but also room for turning away from the things we held close.

Now, let me clarify again. Here's what I'm *not* saying: "Sure, a brutal leader or spiritual environment traumatized you or even abused you, but really it's your fault for expecting them to have integrity and act in Christlike ways. You should have just expected them to violate you. Don't worry about it, I suppose Jesus will deal with it later." Here's what I *am* saying: "In the daily grind of sinners walking through the Christian life in proximity to one another, you're going to feel disappointed by people and even leaders. You're going to get hurt by them sometimes, and so are they by you. Seeing Jesus as the only truly Good Shepherd (instead of expecting everyone else to be that for you) will help you bear with the failings of others (and yourself!). With *Jesus* as the Good Shepherd, both your leaders and you have room to be fallen humans with one another. (And in the end, if a situation moves from a normal hardship in the Christian life to something truly heinous—like abuse of any kind, covering of sin, or harsh leadership—relocate to a safe pasture, report it, and there's no question—Scripture is clear, Jesus *will* deal with it himself.)[3]

Turning to Hope

I've never been one for the outdoors. This is probably why shepherd imagery fails to land on me. I live in the suburbs and avoid animals at all costs. So, I need help understanding how the shepherds and sheep imagery are metaphors for our faith.

In his book *A Shepherd's Look at Psalm 23*, W. Phillip Keller, says this about the psalm:

> David, in this psalm, is speaking not as a shepherd, though he was one, but as a sheep. One of the flock. He spoke with a strong sense of pride and devotion and admiration. It was as though he literally boasted aloud, "Look at who my shepherd is—my owner—my manager! The Lord is! After all, he knew from firsthand experience that the lot in life of any particular sheep depended on the type of man who owned it. Some men were kind, gentle, intelligent, brave, and selfless in their devotion to their stock. Under one man sheep would struggle, starve, and suffer endless hardship. In another's care they would flourish and thrive contentedly. So if the Lord is my Shepherd I should know something of His character and understand something of His ability.[4]

In Psalm 23 we get the embodiment of this Good Shepherd. When Jesus tells the man born blind (and all who surround him) that he's the Good Shepherd, this is what he has in mind.

Let's look at this famous psalm, even though it's likely familiar to you. If John 9–10 isn't enough to show us just how faithful he is to his sheep, Psalm 23 (ESV) comes to us in poetry to drive it home. I bet you could recite it from memory now. "The LORD is my shepherd . . ." you know the rest.

> *I shall not want.*

This can be translated as: "I have what I need." Perhaps this helps explain it more clearly. Of course, we want for stuff, right? *I want a new pair of shoes. I want to eat tacos for dinner. I want to get more sleep at night. I want to be able to pay for college for my kids.* But what if I don't get those things? Is Jesus a bad shepherd? We might "want" for stuff, but we need nothing. If we don't have it, we didn't need it.

The Good Shepherd never leaves his people lacking in their needs being met—even if our desires tell us otherwise. The man born blind lost a lot of things when he gained his sight. Surely, he wanted for many things—namely parents who defended him and a synagogue to call his church home. But when you have the Good Shepherd, you have everything, even if your hands come up empty and your friends have all scattered.

> *He makes me lie down in green pastures. He leads me besides still waters. He restores my soul.*

This is so much abundance, right? It's the proof that we have what we need. Sheep are known for being helpless and defenseless. There is a reason God uses sheep as the image for describing his people. No amount of feeling self-sufficient removes the reality that we're finite beings who control nothing.

And yet, the Good Shepherd is always watching, always guiding, always leading us to places of rest and restoration. He takes needy, dependent people and gently takes us where we need to go—even if we don't see at the moment that this is for our good. There is a lot in our life that is uncertain. Even as I write, Israel and Palestine are at war, and Ukraine is still being invaded by Russia. The world is not at peace. Our lives are not at peace. But the presence of the Good Shepherd means peace is possible. And the next verse shows us that it's possible no matter what we're walking through.

> *He leads me in paths of righteousness for his name's sake.*

Have you ever wondered what was the right next step? Have you ever struggled to have victory over a specific sin, weighed down by your repeated return back to your old patterns? Me too. The Good Shepherd knows this about us and leads us on paths that make us more like himself. But sheep are stubborn creatures, both figuratively and literally. Sheep don't like to change. They want to stay on old paths and in old habits. He takes us where we don't always want to go so we can become who he wants us to be. Bad shepherds might force us into obedience through coercion or legalism. But the Good Shepherd is a gentle guide, pointing us toward what is best for us. All around us, life can be a raging ocean of suffering, loss, pain, and turmoil, but peace is possible and righteousness can be ours because he walks with us.

> *Even though I walk through the valley of the shadow of death, I will fear no evil, for you are with me.*

Jesus never promises that suffering won't come. In fact, the bulk of the New Testament is written to suffering Christians about the suffering they are experiencing. First Peter is written to exiled Christians living under Roman rule. Romans 8 is a reminder that suffering won't have the last word. Second Corinthians 4 speaks of the fruit of suffering in our lives. Suffering is expected. But in our suffering Jesus promises something better—his presence.

Keller goes on to write, "In the Christian's life there is no substitute for the keen awareness that my Shepherd is nearby. There is nothing like Christ's presence to dispel the fear, the panic, the terror of the unknown."[5] There is a lot to be afraid of, and walking through the dark valley of death tops the list. But even when we pass through the waters of death, Christ is with us (Isa. 43:2).

Jesus will promise later in John that he is sending the Holy Spirit to remain with his people (John 14). Suffering has a way of isolating us. Disappointment from leaders leaves us bereft of insight and direction. But the Good Shepherd sticks close even through the darkest valleys. Like he came to the man born blind after he had been cast out of the temple, he also comes to us and asks us to trust him. He walks beside us through every dark valley we face—never abandoning us.

Your rod and your staff, they comfort me.

Discipline is a hard topic in our modern culture. We like to be free. But here, David talks about two forms of comfort: the rod and the staff. The rod is used to protect the sheep from animals who could kill them, and to correct the sheep when they stray.[6] The staff is used to guide the sheep toward right living.

The Good Shepherd disciplines, protects, and guides. He roots out our sin and provides us with a path forward. It's the kindness of the Lord that leads us to obedience and faithfulness. It's his discipline that protects us from making a mess of our lives. If you're tempted to walk away from the path of righteousness, the staff comes to lead you back and the rod disciplines you when you refuse to turn. The best thing for us is that God doesn't leave us to our own devices, and he will not lose a single sheep.

> *You prepare a table before me in the presence of my enemies; you anoint my head with oil; my cup overflows.*

There are times where we are faced with injustice and those who reject Christ. We see evil winning, and we wonder if we've made the wrong choice—or worse, if God can be trusted. Here is a reminder that justice will prevail. We're taken back to abundance again. In this context, they couldn't go to the store to buy more oil. They couldn't have a feast at a table every single day. It was a special occasion to both have a cup overflowing and a feast at a table. To make it even more compelling, this is a table in the presence of his enemies. God shows David that evil does not win. Isn't that comforting when we're tempted to think that bad shepherds hold all the cards? David reminds us that one day justice will prevail. Whatever we lack in the moment of our suffering will one day be reversed by the Good Shepherd.

> *Surely goodness and mercy shall follow me all the days of my life, and I shall dwell in the house of the* Lord *forever.*

This is the culmination of everything Psalm 23 has just mentioned. The Christian Standard Bible says: "Only goodness and faithful love will pursue me" (v. 6). In seasons where it's hard to see the Good Shepherd, we need these verses close to our hearts. When it doesn't feel like goodness and faithful love are following us. When it actually feels like evil and hatred are our closest allies. The Good Shepherd never falls asleep on the job.

In every instance of being let down, we're tempted to think there is rot at the root and nothing can be trusted. But remember, for this man born blind in John 9, all he had were these religious leaders before he met Jesus. Jesus wasn't the problem, the corruption was.

I have seen leaders rise and fall too many times. I've seen people training for ministry shipwreck their lives over unrepentant sin. I've sat with friends confused over the direction their pastors are going. I've sat with men and women broken over the dissolution of their marriages.

Of course, I have witnessed phenomenal pastors and leaders too. But the sad reality is their stories are not the ones you replay on a mental loop. They may lead to your health, but the undoing that bad leadership and broken relationships bring takes far longer to untangle. One bad shepherd can undo a lifetime of good ones.

Leaders represent Christ to the people. In Ezekiel's day, they were God's mouthpiece. In our day, they can carry such "Godlike" power and influence that it's hard for us to distinguish between our heavenly Father and the man in the pulpit or the woman on the screen. The same can be said of our parents, ministry leaders, teachers, and even spouses.

This is where John 10 comes with such power. Other shepherds may come at us with bad leadership, but Christ never does. Other shepherds may abandon us, but Christ stays closer than a brother. Other shepherds may malign our character, but Christ speaks words of comfort—more than that, he defends and advocates for us in the face of failure or false accusation. Other shepherds may disappoint us, even mistreat us but Christ—the Good Shepherd—holds out abundant life to us. He will not abandon his sheep. He didn't in his greatest moment of suffering on the cross, and he won't now as he's interceding for you before the throne of his Father.

Over the last two decades, I have had to send those words to friends far too many times. I have also had to say those words to myself. Jesus doesn't say these things to us simply to provide something better to emulate. He gives us these words knowing we will never measure up to his standards. His words are a comfort to a people who look at the landscape and know that everyone else will at some point hurt them or disappoint them. The man born blind was abandoned by everyone he trusted for aligning with Jesus.

Sometimes we are too. But Jesus finds us in our isolation and says "I'm the Good Shepherd. I won't betray you. I am someone to believe in."

6

He Is with You

(John 13–16)

My senior year of high school, our world was rocked when our beloved choir director needed open heart surgery. Minutes into first period, an all-call announcement came over the loudspeaker. Every Acapella choir member needed to head to the auditorium for a meeting. We were days away from the biggest local competition of the year, followed by our annual trip for more competitions. When we returned, we jumped into our spring performances with weeks of extra practices. We needed him. We depended on him. We didn't know how to perform without him.

Instead, crowded onto risers in the school auditorium, he looked in our faces—eager high schoolers who adored him—and told us he was having by-pass surgery the next day. We were crushed. Few of us even knew what heart surgery meant. We were still kids, with young grandparents and very few problems. All we knew is that our fearless leader wouldn't accompany us to our competitions, and potentially wouldn't be back before the end of the school year. There were tears, anger, and mostly confusion. *Who would direct us? How would we go on without him at the helm?*

I imagine the disciples experienced fears and tears (though on a much grander scale) as Jesus told them he was leaving them. Had they paid attention, they would have understood this was the plan all along. But when we find them in the farewell discourse in John 13–16, you'd think it was their first hearing of Jesus's impending departure. And he wasn't just leaving them for open heart surgery. He was leaving them to die a violent and humiliating death. But even in his resurrection he would leave them again. All their hopes for him staying on earth to establish his kingdom right then were dashed. They were understandably confused. They needed a plan.

They needed hope.

Unlike the disciples, we've never seen God in the flesh. Jesus hasn't walked among us, eaten meals with us, or lived life with us. We haven't witnessed him perform miracles and we haven't heard his voice.

But, like the disciples, we sometimes feel his absence. In feeling his absence, we're afraid. And the fear leads us to doubt his care, or even our own faith.

For the disciples, everything Jesus tells them wasn't in their plan for the kingdom. He's also been their closest friend these last three years—and now he's leaving them. It's almost too much for them to take in, and you hear it in their confused questions. They're straining for hope.

As Jesus prepares to leave his friends, he gives them parting words. And he answers their questions.

How do you believe when you can't see him, experience him, or understand his work? How do you believe when you feel like he's left you?

John unpacks it for us.

The Presence of Christ (Promised Holy Spirit)

The entire farewell discourse in John 13–16 is one distressing revelation after another. The disciples were confused and frightened when Jesus told them his departure was imminent. He does the unexpected in washing their feet. He prepares them for his death and burial, by serving them in a lowly way—taking on the form of a slave to wipe dirt and animal excrement from them. They find out one of their close friends is going to betray Jesus. Peter's denial is predicted by Jesus, which shocks him and leads to a classic Peter response—"there's no way this is happening, Jesus." Jesus tells them that this dinner is the last one for a while. He's got to leave them, both to die and to go back to his Father. The blows in this scene keep coming. And the anxiety rises.

Everything about the Savior confuses them. They expected his kingdom to come in power and authority. The reality of the kingdom was humble service and giving up his life.

Like any scared child, they're filled with questions.

What is surprising about this promise from Jesus is that he tells them it's actually better for them if he leaves them (John 16:7). This entire scene is circular, meaning Jesus repeats himself. If you're a parent, or ever spent time with children, you know that just because you tell them something once, doesn't mean it sticks. Especially in a crisis, they need regular reminders about what's expected and what's to come. The disciples are no different than children. *We are no different than children.*

Knowing their distress, Jesus tells them what is coming. He begins by saying that his departure is not a crisis. Instead, it's the way he's going to care for them in his absence. In John 14:16–17, Jesus says: "I will ask the Father, and he will give you another Counselor to be with you forever. He is the Spirit of truth. The world is unable to receive him because it doesn't see him or know him. But you do know him, because he remains with you and will be in you." Then right after this he says one of my favorite lines in all of John—"I will not leave you as orphans; I am coming to you" (v. 18). The disciples are reeling from the news of Jesus's departure, and Jesus prepares them by saying "I'm still going to be with you."

This is a theme he comes back to repeatedly in John 13–16. There are multiple ways John's word for the Holy Spirit is translated. The Greek word is *paraclete*, while some translate it as "advocate" or "helper." The Christian Standard Bible translates him as "Counselor." But there's an important word added before and that's "another." In essence, Jesus is saying "another like me is going to come alongside you, just as I've been walking alongside you all these years." The point is that the Counselor, who is the Holy Spirit, is the same deity as Jesus Christ. Jesus has been their helper while on earth, as God in the flesh. The Spirit of Jesus Christ will be their helper in his physical absence, indwelling them forever. Jesus is with them, and his impending death and departure grieves them. But Jesus comforts them with this promise: *I'm sending you someone who is the same as me. I'm sending you another person of the Godhead. I'm sending you myself.*

What grieved them was the loss they knew was coming. What should comfort them is that there is no gap in coverage. The Spirit of the Lord Jesus Christ will always be with them. Andreas Köstenberger writes, "Jesus strenuously argues that his physical presence will be replaced with the Spirit's continual spiritual presence, which knows no limits in time and space."[1] Jesus repeatedly says throughout the farewell discourse that his departure is for their good. The Spirit's arrival is better than having him there in the flesh. But it's largely because it's the fulfillment of what God intended for his people from the very beginning.

There are a lot of thoughts about the Spirit in modern evangelicalism. I've heard people joke that the Holy Spirit is the "forgotten person of the Trinity." In the Baptist circles I've often been in, we don't talk about the Spirit as much as we do God the Son and God the Father.

But the Spirit is the third person of the Godhead—the Trinity. He is God. Michael Reeves says this about the Trinity, "While distinct persons, [they] are absolutely inseparable from each other. Not confused, but undividable. They are who they are *together.* They always *are* together, and thus they always *work* together."[2] Reeves goes on to write, "The Spirit's personal presence in us means we are brought to enjoy the Spirit's own intimate communion with the Father and the Son. If the Spirit were not God, he could not do that. It is all because God is three persons—Father, Son, and Spirit—that we can have such communion. If God was in heaven and his Spirit a mere force, he would be more distant than the moon."[3]

The Spirit is God in the same way the Father and Son are God. He is, as the Nicene Creed states, "the Lord, the giver of life, who proceeds from the Father and the Son. With the Father and the Son he is worshipped and glorified."[4] This is what Jesus promises in this section of John. God came to them in the flesh in Jesus Christ, and he is staying with them through the Holy Spirit. The Father, Son, and Spirit do not operate outside of each other, and God's intent has always been to dwell with his people.

John writes about the Word being the agent of creation. He was in the beginning and all things were created through him and by him. But the Spirit is not missing from the picture at the dawn of creation. In Genesis 1:2, Moses writes that "the Spirit of God was hovering over the surface of the waters." This was all right before God said, "Let there be light."

God's presence among his creation and his people has always been his intention. He walked among his people in the garden (Gen. 3:8). He appeared as a pillar of cloud and fire in the wilderness, guiding his people safely through the Exodus and wandering

(Exod. 13:17–14:29). He inhabited the tabernacle and later the temple (Exod. 25:8; 2 Chronicles 7). Then he came in the flesh in the incarnation. As we saw in chapter 1, Bible scholars Duvall and Hays argue that "God's relational presence" is the central theme of the entire Bible. Nowhere do we see this more clearly than in the gospel, they say, "The goal of the gospel is not simply salvation or deliverance from evil but also eternal communion with God, the Creator and Redeemer and Sustainer."[5]

But up to this point, this was never permanent. God's people needed a path back to him that lasted. They needed him to consistently dwell among them, guiding them, sustaining them, and caring for them. Jesus says, in essence, "I'm sending you the Spirit, and he will keep you all the way to the end." James M. Hamilton says that the Spirit is the "guarantee that they will enjoy God's presence forever."[6] Thinking back to what John writes in John 1, that Son came to earth to "tabernacle" with us. Now the Son sends the Spirit to "tabernacle" inside us. What kind of God goes to such lengths to be with—and now *in*—his people?

This God—who is someone to believe in.

In the final moments of his life on earth, Jesus looks away from himself and toward his scared disciples and essentially says, "I will be with you, even when it won't always feel like it." He tells them he won't leave them as orphans because they were going to feel like orphans. Imagine their situation for a moment. They've sat down to dinner with Jesus, not unlike other meals with him. Lazarus has recently been raised from the dead, and they watched him walk out of the tomb. They saw a blind man regain sight. They watched lost people come to faith. They experienced intimate communion with Jesus. He was their leader, but he was also their friend. And now he tells them he must go away. How else would they feel except like orphaned children, with no compass to guide them or keel to stabilize them.

There was a lot of unknown ahead. This is why they needed the Spirit to "remind them of everything" he told them (John 14:26). It's why they needed the Spirit to give them peace (John 14:27–29). It's why they needed the Spirit to convict them. It's why they needed the Spirit to help them to obey. It's why they needed the comfort that even if Jesus wasn't by their side, they had something better—he was "tabernacling" inside them. Every effort to regain relational presence with God failed or was temporary. Jesus had to leave them, so the Spirit could come to restore what was lost in Eden. God was coming back to stay—inside his wayward people, making a way back for them again. They didn't see how it was a comfort, but it was the answer to the ache that had plagued God's people since Adam and Eve were cast out of the garden. They were made to live in constant communion with God, but sin kept him at a distance. Now Jesus was telling them that his Spirit was taking up residence inside of them.

There is a peace that comes when the Spirit takes up residence inside you. In the same way there is no gap in coverage between Jesus's departure and the Spirit's indwelling, there is also no gap in coverage between belief and life in the Spirit. To be a believer is to have the Spirit with you always. Sometimes we sense it, and other times we can't locate his work. But it's helpful for us to acknowledge times we know he is working in and through us, because we need these moments to carry us when he seems far off.

I first met Kim at a retreat for moms who lost babies to miscarriage or stillbirth. When I met her, we had both lost two babies, though now her losses are at four. Her resolute hope through repeat grief inspires me, but as I talked to her, I was struck by how the promises of Jesus ring as true in our modern world as they did thousands of years ago.

Jesus tells his disciples that one benefit of the Spirit's presence is that he will bring to mind all that Jesus taught them (John 14:26). In other words, he will bring to mind the very words of Christ. Kim writes:

> I knew I desperately needed God's peace. Immediately, John 14 came to my mind as the chapter in the Bible in which Jesus told his disciples that he was going to leave them his peace, a peace that is unlike the world's peace. I opened my Bible to John chapter 14 and started reading from the beginning for context: "Let not your hearts be troubled. Believe in God; believe also in me" [ESV]. I read Jesus's words that he spoke to his disciples, that he was going to prepare a place for them and would return to take them to himself (vv. 2–3). I read Thomas's uncertainty about where Jesus was going and Jesus's assurance that he himself is the way to the Father (vv. 5–6). As I continued reading, I was struck by verse 19, "Yet a little while and the world will see me no more, but you will see me. Because I live, you also will live." In that moment, the reality of eternal life became tangible to me. I saw the hopelessness of the world no longer seeing Jesus contrasted with the disciples' assurance of seeing Jesus again. I felt reassured that I, like the disciples, would see Jesus in his eternal home one day. I continued reading to the end of the chapter. I was encouraged by the thought that the Holy Spirit would remind Jesus's disciples of his words

> (v. 26), as he had done for me that very morning by bringing John 14 to mind. I read the verse that led me to John 14:27, "Peace I leave with you; my peace I give to you. Not as the world gives do I give to you. Let not your hearts be troubled, neither let them be afraid."

There was a lot to be frightened in that moment. Kim still had to deliver her dead baby. But the Spirit's presence in her life anchored her, brought the Word to mind, and assured her that she was not alone. He had not left her as an orphan. He stayed with her in her grief by revealing his Word to her.

She went on to write, "Eleven days after finding out there was no heartbeat, I delivered our son, Quinn Zoe, at home on July 7, 2019. We buried him in the children's section of the cemetery where many of my relatives are buried. Quinn's headstone is engraved with the second sentence of John 14:19, 'Because I live, you will live also.'"

Like the disciples, the reality of her loss (and the impending birth of her stillborn child), led to fear and feelings of abandonment. *What good can come out of such horrible suffering?* But Jesus tells us in John 14:29, "I have told you now before it happens so that when it does happen *you may believe*." He's left no stone unturned in preparing his people for a lifetime of his physical absence. He came to live in his people by the Holy Spirit—to be an ever-present reminder of his care, conviction, and comfort.

All they could comprehend in this moment was what was immediately in front of them. The loss seemed too great. Even for Kim, looking at her circumstances alone seemed like all hope was lost. But Jesus loves us all the way to the end and gives us his presence as a continual reminder that he has not forgotten us—even when all signs point elsewhere.

When Jesus wants to comfort his friends, he tells them that he's coming to them. But this leads to an even deeper reality that is linked to his presence among us.

Union with Christ (The Greatest Hope in All the World)

After Jesus promises his disciples that they won't be alone when he leaves them, he unpacks what this looks like. To do this, he uses a word picture they would have understood.

I've tried to have a garden for the last few summers. In theory, I love the idea. Every time I watered my plants or pulled weeds, I found so many metaphors for the Christian life. As a writer and teacher, I understand why the garden imagery works. But as I've mentioned before, I was not gifted with a green thumb, nor a love for the outdoors. To make a garden work, you need both. You need to instinctively understand what is happening when your tomato plants are overgrown with vines but no fruit. Or at a minimum you need to possess a desire to Google it. You also need to be okay with standing outside in the heat of summer to nurture your plants. You need to find ways to protect them from rabbits and squirrels. You need to be content to pull caterpillars and other bugs off your tender leaves. Unfortunately, I'm not a person equipped with this sort of contentment. The only time I like being outside is when it's 75 degrees or I'm at the pool. Otherwise, I like the theory of a garden, not the practice of gardening.

Thankfully, God is not that kind of gardener.

In John 15, Jesus continues his departing encouragements to his disciples. After telling them he won't leave them as "orphans," he promises to remain with them through the Holy Spirit. As he continues to unpack what this promise means for them, he gives them assurance that this is not a temporary residency.

Consider the Spirit's work up to this point in their experience. The cloud and pillar of fire went away. The Spirit left the temple. But now, the Spirit comes to stay because he's sent by the Father and the Son. Jesus introduces another "I am" statement in John 15 to drive it home. He says:

> "I am the true vine, and my Father is the gardener. Every branch in me that does not produce fruit he removes, and prunes every branch that produces fruit so that it will produce more fruit. You are already clean because of the word I have spoken to you. Remain in me, and I in you. Just as a branch is unable to produce fruit by itself unless it remains on the vine, neither can you unless you remain in me. I am the vine; you are the branches. The one who remains in me and I in him produces much fruit, because you can do nothing without me." (vv. 1–5)

They have the promise of the Spirit's indwelling, now they have the image of his indwelling. When the Spirit takes up residence in a believer, he unites us to the Son. We are so intricately connected to him that we are like branches on a vine. Every move the vine makes, the branch makes with it. The branch grows and bears fruit because of the life-giving vine. The branch is nourished and sustained by the vine. The same is true with our union with Christ. The life he lives, we now live. This is a theme that is picked up repeatedly in the New Testament.

I've always found it interesting that during a discourse on being the vine and us being the branches Jesus uses a mixed metaphor. He says, "You are already clean" (v. 3).[7] But branches have no need of cleansing. Why not say something else that fits with the metaphor? I think Jesus is intentional here in throwing in this statement on their cleanness, and it makes sense in understanding our union with Christ. In Ephesians 1, Paul explains this further. He uses the phrase "in him," and says that "in him we have redemption through his blood, the forgiveness of our trespasses" (v. 7). In other words, we've been made clean. But then he follows the progression of our union saying we've been "sealed with the promised Holy Spirit" who was given as a "down payment of our inheritance" (vv. 13–14). Being part of the vine means you're already clean. You're already part of the plant. This is an important implication before Jesus talks about bearing fruit because it leaves no question about how Jesus saves. He saves through his blood so we will bear fruit. Not the other way around.

Jen Wilkin says that our union with Christ enables us to "become who we were meant to be."[8] We were meant to be holy. We were meant to dwell with God. We were meant to live as his representatives in the world. Jesus Christ is the exact imprint of his nature—the perfect embodiment of the image of God. And through the Spirit we have the presence of the Son in us.

He is God recreating us into the image we were meant to show all along. This only happens by abiding in the vine—Jesus Christ.

Michael Reeves says this about our union with Christ:

> What a far cry from the exhausting idea that Christ has done his bit and now it's time to do ours! We are not chained to the task of trying to pay back the huge debt we owe him. We are united to the Son so we can enter into his life. Our joy, our prayers, our mission, our holiness, our suffering, our hope: all are *participation* in the life of the Son. We are not simply given some *thing* called "eternal life" and then sent out to get on with it.

> *We* are not forerunners with final responsibility.
> He is the firstborn; we live in his slipstream.[9]

Branches are useless on their own. If that sounds discouraging to you, ask yourself what other hope you have for growth? How overwhelmed do you feel each day, trying to be good enough on your own? What's your track record? You might be able to try it for a while, but everyone falls at some point. But Jesus says that he's doing everything for you. He's the way you grow. All you must do is abide in his life-giving vine.

Go back to John 1 in your mind. What kind of God comes to live among his wayward people? The incarnation is astounding, but how much more the Spirit's indwelling us? He's so committed to us that he makes us clean by his perfect life in our place, then he takes up residency in us—the new temple—so he can rest assured we will make it all the way home. Don't you want assurance to come from outside of yourself? We've all spent time trying to be good enough, or produce fruit in our own strength, and that can only last for so long before we miss the mark or burn out. Union with Christ—abiding in the vine—is an invitation to rest. Everything Christ receives as the perfect Son of God is ours. His righteousness is our righteousness. We no longer need to strive to maintain our own standing before him. His home is our home because we're part of his family. His relationship with the Father is our relationship with the Father, and we can approach him boldly because of Christ. The Spirit is the assurance that what Christ inherits, we will receive in glory. There is no gap in presence and there is no gap in inheritance.

Assurance from Christ (Fruit of the Spirit's Work)

But how do we know it is working? Peter heard these words from Jesus, and yet within a matter of hours he denied him. Thomas was there in the garden that night, but when Jesus rose from the dead, he doubted. Philip heard Jesus speak and still asked for more proof. We come to a crossroads where fruit is scarce and doubt creeps in.

The Spirit's presence is a comfort on multiple fronts. He comforts us to know we aren't alone. He comforts us to know that we're united to Christ and what's his is ours. But he also comforts us to know that the work he began in us he will complete (Phil. 1:6). In other words, he knows how to garden. John 15:1 says that the Father is the gardener, and like any good gardener he prunes his branches so more fruit can grow. He tailors his gardening for maximum growth.

It's counterintuitive, but it works.

Like I said, I'm not a gardener. But one year we tried our hand at tomatoes. For most of the summer, the vines were abundant, but the fruit was nonexistent. I shared a picture of my plants on Instagram and joked that I'm not good at keeping plants going. Someone commented that I needed to prune my plants (who knew?!) and that would probably help foster growth. I got to work, cutting back my tomato plant as a last-ditch effort to make the garden count for something. Wouldn't you know, it worked. Within weeks I had flowers budding and then soon tomatoes emerged. But when I was cutting back those branches, my novice gardener brain told me, "You're killing these plants." Pruning feels like death. A pruned plant looks like a barren tree. Sometimes for a long time. But cutting back dead branches allows the real fruit to grow. The work is happening in the roots—in the *vine*.

The same is true in the Christian life. We must talk about union with Christ before we talk about fruit, otherwise we will think that seasons of seeming fruitlessness means we aren't truly saved. There is a time and place to talk about a fruitless existence for the Christian. But Jesus's point here is to assure his disciples that they will bear fruit if they are united to him, so when the pruning comes, they don't doubt that God's given up on them. If they are abiding in the vine—united to Christ—it's impossible for him to forsake them. They are part of him now.

Pruning is confusing, and the effects of pruning can last a long time. My tomato plant caught on quickly, but my crape myrtles are barren every winter for months before the branches grow back. Depending on the nature of the plant, the timeline varies in the pruning process. I think this is why Jesus tells them about it before the pruning comes. We need the truth before the trial, or we will lose our footing when it comes. We will forget what he's done for us and is doing in us.

Sometimes You See Him, Sometimes You Don't

One of my favorite scenes in the Chronicles of Narnia comes at the end of *The Voyage of the Dawn Treader*. If you're familiar with the story, you know that at the end of the book Lucy and Edmund prepare to leave Narnia and are told they can't return. Like their older siblings, they're now too old to come to Narnia. As they talk to Aslan, they weep over the realization that coming back to Narnia is not possible. Like the disciples, they're heartbroken.

> "You are too old, children," said Aslan, "and you must begin to come close to your own world now."
>
> "It isn't Narnia, you know," sobbed Lucy. "It's *you*. We shan't meet *you* there. And how can we live, never meeting you?"
>
> "But you shall meet me, dear one," said Aslan.
>
> "Are—are you there too, Sir?" said Edmund.
>
> "I am," said Aslan. "But there I have another name. You must learn to know me by that name. This was the very reason why you were brought to

> Narnia, that by knowing me here for a while, you may know me better there."[10]

They were given a glimpse of him in Narnia, so they had something to hold on to in their world. They needed to see him as believable there, so they had the faith to see him at home. But this comfort of his presence was not in isolation. Aslan had spent years preparing Lucy and Edmond for this moment, but it didn't make it any less painful. The departure of Aslan leads to an ache inside them, which is the ache we all feel as we long to be with Christ. Until then, we're comforted by his presence, the Holy Spirit. Aslan is a picture of the biblical Jesus, and if Aslan didn't leave Lucy and Edmond as orphans, how much more can we trust the true Christ hasn't left us? The comfort Lucy and Edmond needed was that even when they couldn't "see" him, he hadn't ever left them. For most of us, that's the story of our Christian experience. We get a glimpse of him sometimes, but that's going to have to carry us until we see him again. We walk by faith—belief.

But then there are times where he shows up in the fire.

If you spent any time in children's church as a kid, you remember the story of the three men in the fiery furnace. Shadrach, Meshach, and Abednego were flannelgraph staples in my class as a child, but I always understood the story from the perspective of courage (which they no doubt possessed). But the point of the story is not their courage. It's that they weren't alone. Dale Ralph Davis writes,

> Christ's flock are strangely comforted here. Christ did not keep them out of the furnace, but found them in it. He does not always shield you from all distresses and dangers, but it is in the loneliness, in the betrayal, in the loss that the Fourth Man comes and walks with you. He has the knack of

> both exposing you to, yet keeping you through, waters and rivers of fire (cf. Isa. 43:2–3)—and operating rooms and funeral parlours and an empty house. The Fourth Man can always find his people.[11]

From the beginning of time until now, the Fourth Man—Jesus Christ—finds his people and stays with them. Sometimes we sense he's with us, a lot of the times we're carried forward on belief. Like Lucy and Edmund, we have memories of his presence to sustain us when the reality of life screams that he's left us as orphans. But if we remember, we see that while he is not with us in the flesh any longer, he's given us his Spirit to live inside us, conforming us to the image of himself and bringing us all the way home. There is no gap in coverage.

The news about our beloved choir director was distressing, especially for high school students. But he didn't leave us unprepared. When he announced his surgery, he also announced his replacement—an equally beloved teacher who had recently returned from maternity leave. We weren't left in the lurch. In his absence, we had his equal guiding us.

The analogy breaks down because, well, all analogies do. But we're often like the three men in the furnace—doing the next right thing, unsure when assurance of God's presence will come. But if you're his, he will find you.

Shadrach, Meshach, and Abednego were thrown down into the furnace, believing the only way out was in a body bag. Yet they trusted the promise of God's deliverance and care. How much more do we have assurance? We have everything Jesus promised in John 13–16, and centuries of proof that "the Fourth Man always finds his people"—more than that, dwells *in* them.

7

He Is Praying for You

(John 17)

A FEW YEARS AGO, I listened to the audiobook of *The Only Plane in the Sky*, an oral history of the events of September 11, 2001. Story after story is told from the vantage point of people who both survived the attack and those who never made it home. Every word of the book is taken from interviews of survivors and transcripts from phone calls and 911 recordings. And you can hear the agony in their words. You can sense the fear. For many, it's the last recorded words we have from them. For others, their most traumatic moments captured in our national history.

You can imagine what scared people say when they call family and friends. A finance intern beginning his career, calls his mom to tell her he's okay, but he loves her. A flight attendant calls her husband with regular updates, assuring him they have a plan for survival. A family traveling across the country for a big move calls grandparents back home to find out what was happening on the ground. Every conversation held purpose. If a few moments are all you have, you make the words count.

For those in the air, and on the upper floors in the World Trade Center, what began as confused calls urging everyone to stay calm eventually moved to a realization that they weren't coming down the stairs alive. Some had mere minutes before the line went dead, but they made sure to say things like:

> "I love you."
>
> "These were the best years of my life."
>
> "Please tell the kids I love them and am proud of them."

Many families saved these messages forever, not wanting to erase the last words of their lost family members.

What would you say if you had moments left to live? In John 17, we read exactly how Jesus answers the question.

Jesus knows this is his final moment with his friends (John 16:16). Two chapters later, Judas brings the crowd to arrest Jesus (18:3). Jesus has no illusion about what is to come. Death is on the horizon. Judgment for sin awaits him. And instead of looking inward, he looks outward to his scared disciples and prays for them.

We know from the other Gospels, that more happens this night than just the words exchanged in John 13–16 and Jesus's high priestly prayer in John 17. We know that Jesus is troubled about what is to come (Matt. 26:38). In Matthew 26:36–46 and in Mark 14:32–43, Jesus takes James, John, and Peter to the garden of Gethsemane to pray with him. They fall asleep, and Jesus cries out in agony for deliverance. He's clearly shaken and overcome with grief about facing impending death, abandonment from his friends, and wrath poured out for our sin.

And yet, of all John could include about this highly charged moment in Jesus's life, what John wants us to see about the Savior is that he prays for us. Moments before his arrest, he prays for his scared disciples—and for you and me.

Let's look at his prayer together.

He Prays for Himself

John 17 is often called the "High Priestly Prayer." The writer of Hebrews calls Jesus the "Great High Priest," the one who is better than the human high priests who came before him (Heb. 4:14–16). Jesus prays for his friends, and all who come after him, on the night before Passover. On the night before the Passover lamb is slaughtered, the one who is the Lamb of God is also the one who advocates for God's people as the Great High Priest. There are no lengths too great that he will not go for his people.

But in this moment, Jesus knows that everything he came to accomplish is on the horizon. All throughout John's Gospel, Jesus maintains that his "hour" has not come. In John 2, he says to his mother his hour has not come when she asks him to make his power known at the wedding at Cana. In John 7, he slips away from an angry crowd because John tells us, "His hour had not yet come" (v. 30). It carries more theological weight than saying, "It's not the right time for Jesus to die."

When Jesus speaks of his hour, he is purposeful. It speaks to his control and his authority. In John 2, he was not ready to show his full power to everyone, so he says it's not his hour. And in John 7, he refuses to be controlled. If someone or some group could control his hour, then he would cease to be God. But now, he's ready. His hour is here, he is in full control of it, and it has a specific purpose—to take away the sins of the world in a way that the blood of bulls and goats could never do. He came to bring God's wayward people back into the Father's presence.

When he prays for himself in John 17:1–5, he prays for his glory. In this prayer, Jesus repeats familiar themes in John, but also familiar themes in Scripture. When we think of glory, we think of someone who is clamoring for the limelight. They beg to be noticed. But that's not how God thinks of glory, at least not for himself. Glory is rightly due him because he's God. But glory also is the revelation of his character. When Moses asks to see God's glory in Exodus 33, God tells him that is impossible. Moses has just interceded for the people after they rebelled in worship of the golden calf. Even during their rebellion, God assures them he will be with them. His presence will always go before them and dwell among them (v. 14). But Moses wants to see God's glory. He wants to see God in all his fullness. Moses has experienced God's mercy in his forgiveness of the wayward Israelite people. Moses has talked with God and received his commandments. Now he wants more. Wouldn't we all want more? What Moses asks for is impossible, and God knew this.

God had another way, so he hid his full glory from Moses, but allowed him to see a glimpse. God tells Moses that he will let him see his goodness, but it's only from a distance. He will proclaim his name and his glory in front of Moses, but it will be veiled because he will also hide Moses in the crevice of a rock. And what he revealed was his gracious, abounding in love, long-suffering, merciful, kindness to his people. In other words, God's glory is so magnificent that the weight would crush Moses. But even at a distance Moses marvels at what he beholds.

Jesus prays that his disciples, and all who come after, would see *this* glory—the glory that Moses only saw dimly, but that the Son sees continually in the presence of the Father. Jesus prays that all would see God in all his fullness, displayed through his Son, Jesus Christ. What Moses could only view from a cave, Jesus prays we all would see with no restrictions.

In just a matter of hours, they would. The cross, and the subsequent resurrection after it, is the ultimate display of God's character. It shows God is merciful because he sends his Son to die in our place. It shows he's holy because sin must be punished. It shows he's good because he keeps his promise to bring his people back. It shows he's just because he deals with sin by paying for it with the blood of his Son. And it shows not even death can hold him back from finalizing his work. Moses saw dimly, we see fully.

Jesus also prays that through his glory, people would receive eternal life (John 17:2–3). The entire point of the book of John is to show that Jesus is someone for us to believe in. But John is concerned with belief that has both an object and an effect (John 20:31). We were made to live, and when sin entered the world, so did death and punishment for sin. Jesus came to restore us to God. We will talk in other chapters about the home Jesus is making for us (John 14), but in his final moments, Jesus prays that his work to "bring many sons to glory" (as Heb. 2:10 ESV and the hymn beautifully says) would be effective.[1]

This redemptive work that Jesus came to do is fulfilled in a unique way and in a specific moment in time, yes, but it is not something that started during his time on earth. It's a work God began when Adam and Eve fell into sin in Genesis 3. He cast Adam and Eve out of his presence, but he promised to make a way for them to return (Gen. 3:15). Here, Jesus prays for the completion of this effort. He came to finish the work God started in the garden (John 17:4). He came to bring us back to God. All the way to the cross, Jesus's heart is fixed toward his Father and toward the people the Father is giving him. He will not be deterred both in prayer and in action. In praying for himself, he prays for the work that will be accomplished in his death and resurrection, and eventually applied to a great host of others who might believe in it.

He Prays for His Disciples

In the moments before his "hour," he turns his focus to his friends. The disciples are understandably confused and terrified, which we've unpacked in other chapters (chapter 6 and we will see again in chapter 11). His heart for the disciples is one of compassionate care. He had every reason to turn inward only. Suffering awaited him. But he prays for his friends, in their presence. He wants them to hear his heart for them because in his departure they would wonder—*Is he for us? Does he care?* They forever had a prayer in their heart that this is what he wants for them. He prepares them all the way to the end. He prays for three things:

1. Protection
2. Sanctification
3. Set-apart living

Protection

Sadness is on the horizon, but a survey of the book of Acts and the Epistles reveals that the disciples are in for not just sadness, but significant suffering. As we've already seen, at the time John is writing, he would have seen most of his friends die horrific deaths. And John faced persecution too. He spent the remaining years of his life exiled to an island away from everyone. The cost of following Jesus was great, and Jesus knows this. So he prays for protection to fall over his followers—which would include John.

Yes, John's future (along with the future of all the disciples), was about to hit an all-time low with lots of pain, but that doesn't mean Jesus's prayer failed. After all, being protected is different than being insulated. In John 17, Jesus is not asking for his followers to avoid suffering or never endure pain, rather, that they would be protected from ultimate destruction (v. 15). We get a picture of this prayer, and how he protects them in the following verses.

> "I have revealed *your name* to the people you gave me from the world. They were yours, you gave them to me, and they have kept your word. Now they know that everything you have given me is from you, because I have given them the

> words you gave me. They have received them and have known for certain that I came from you. They have believed that you sent me. . . . I pray for them. . . . Holy Father, *protect them by your name* that you have given me." (John 17:6–9a, 11, emphasis added)

In the beginning of John, he tells us that Jesus is the Word made flesh—he is everything God wants to say about himself in a person. We see and know God through the Word, and Jesus is the incarnation of that Word. Scripture progressively reveals God's name, character, and plan of redemption, all culminating in the coming (and rising) of his Son, Jesus Christ. Twice in these verses (vv. 11–12), Jesus asks God to protect his followers by his name. Throughout the Old Testament, God reveals himself to his people. Each time, he tells us more. He drops hints of the Messiah to come. When Jesus is born and walks the earth, he points back to these moments in the Old Testament, telling his people that the Scriptures spoke of him all along the way (Luke 24).

How does knowing God's name protect them? God's name is important in Scripture. In Exodus 3, God appears to Moses in the burning bush. It was a holy experience (he needed to remove his sandals), but up to this point God had not made himself known to Moses. He didn't know what to look for. But when he encountered the burning bush and heard God speak, he knew he was in the presence of holiness (Exod. 3:5).

Later, God commissions Moses to be the mouthpiece and deliverer of his people out of Egyptian slavery and into the promised land (Exod. 3:10). When Moses gets nervous, God reiterates his promise—the promise that has carried him from then until now—he will be with Moses and will be with his people (Exod. 3:12). But Moses wants to know his name. Moses wants credibility backing him not only when he makes such a big ask of Pharaoh, but when the people of Israel wonder why they should trust him to lead them. In a polytheistic culture, Moses knows the first question he's going to get when he demands the release of the Hebrews based on the authority of a certain deity: *which deity?* So, in Exodus 3:13 (ESV), he asks God point-blank to resolve the matter:

> "If I come to the people of Israel and say to them, 'The God of your fathers has sent me to you,' and they ask me, 'What is his name?' what shall I say to them?"

And what does God say?

> God said to Moses, "I AM WHO I AM." And he said, "Say this to the people of Israel: *I* AM has sent me to you." God also said to Moses, "Say this to the people of Israel: '*The LORD*, the God of your fathers, the God of Abraham, the God of Isaac, and the God of Jacob, has sent me to you.' *This is my name forever*, and thus I am to be remembered throughout all generations." (Exod. 3:14–15 ESV, emphasis added)

In other words, "Say, '*I* AM' sent you," Moses. "And if they want an official name, call me by my covenant name: The LORD." (Or, as Israel would have otherwise known it: Yahweh.)

Again, Moses was taking God's message back to Israel living in a pagan land. The Egyptians worshiped multiple gods and they all had names. If Moses was going to be trusted, he had to tell them who sent him. He had to give them a name to set this God apart from all the others. God doesn't play their games, and simply says "I AM WHO I AM." In the same way that God shows Moses his character to explain his presence in Exodus 33, God uses this phrase to explain his identity to Moses and all who come after Moses. There is no one before "I AM" and no one after "I AM." He won't be bothered with trying to explain his name because he's the name above every other name. He's the one who has always existed through the rise and fall of all other rulers, leaders, and false gods.

This phrase for God's name sounds familiar, doesn't it? The Gospel of John is centered around these "I AM" statements. Jesus is the "bread of life; light of the world; true vine; the door; good shepherd; resurrection and the life; and the way, the truth, and the life." All these statements explain in greater detail his identity. God encompasses everything we need, desire, and hope for while needing nothing himself.

God told Moses his name in Midian, Jesus explains God's name by his very existence. The disciples are protected because they know the "I AM." Said another way, the I AM from all the way back in Exodus has appeared before their very eyes—not from a burning bush this time, but in a person. They've seen the I AM in the flesh, heard his words, and they believe (John 17:8).

His name explains his identity, but it also encompasses who he is as God. In John 14–16, Jesus explains that the Trinity works together to preserve and protect the disciples, and all who come after. When we know God's name, we know his identity—and to know God is to know him as Trinity. Jesus prays for himself, but in praying for himself he's praying for all of us. D. A. Carson writes:

> Doubtless Christians in John's day were forced to ponder the implications of this prayer. So also were those who were contemplating the possibility of becoming Christians. The cosmic, spiritual nature of the conflict is laid bare. The followers of Jesus are permitted neither luxury of compromise with a "world" that is intrinsically evil and under the

> devil's power, nor the safety of disengagement. But if the Christian pilgrimage is inherently perilous, the safety that only God himself can provide is assured, as certainly as the prayers of God's own dear Son will be answered.[2]

Jesus prays for the disciples that they would be preserved by knowing God by name—the Great "I AM," the Son and image of this I AM standing in front of them, and the Spirit who will indwell them from this time forward.

Jesus also prays for the Father to protect them from Satan: "I am not praying that you take them out of the world but that you protect them from the evil one" (John 17:15). The disciples have a clear and treacherous enemy working against them as they go forward—an enemy who wants to destroy them and their witness. Peter calls the evil one an "adversary," or put more bluntly, "the devil prowls around like a roaring lion, seeking someone to devour" (1 Pet. 5:8 ESV). The disciples won't be removed from the world in which this enemy roams (as we will see in further detail in the coming verses), but Jesus won't let them be ultimately destroyed. Even if they died for their association with Jesus, they'd come through it and out on the other side in resurrection power—something the enemy had (and has) no power to prevent.

In the coming years, the disciples likely clung to this prayer as they sat in cold prison cells alone, laid with their necks on the chopping block, and cried out in agony in beatings, floggings, and even on an inverted cross. We, too, cling to it in hard times, along with the many other promises in Scripture that "the God of peace will soon crush Satan under your feet" (Rom. 16:20).

Jesus's prayer for their protection builds to his prayer for their sanctification.

Sanctification

As the Word protects them, it also changes them. In his absence, they have the Spirit to guide them and the Word of Christ to direct and sustain them. Now they have Jesus speaking to them in the flesh, but when he's gone, they will rely on the written Word of God. In John 17:17, Jesus says, "Sanctify them by the truth; your word is truth."

In his book *How Sanctification Works*, David Powlison explains sanctification this way:

> Whenever a person makes a turn for the better, *sanctification* is happening . . . Like the word *save*, *sanctify* has a past tense, a present tense, and a future tense.
>
> - In the past tense, your sanctification has already happened—an identity for which you get no credit!
> - In the present tense, your sanctification is now being worked out.
> - In the future tense, your sanctification will be perfected.[3]

This is God's will for us. He's saved us, he is saving us, and he will save us. He's made us new, is making us new, and will make us new. But there is no other way to grow other than staying in God's Word. In John 15, Jesus says that if we abide in the true vine then we will bear fruit. This vine is Jesus Christ, and John says that Jesus is the Word made flesh (John 1).

D. A. Carson writes,

> In practical terms, no-one can be "sanctified" set part for the Lord's use without learning to think

> God's thoughts after him, without learning to live in conformity with the "word" he has graciously given.[4]

As Jesus prays for his friends, he ensures their protection and their growth. Powlison goes on to describe the fruit of our sanctification.

> Perhaps the most dramatic evidence of headway in sanctification is that you no longer think so much about yourself. You are starting to do better when you are not preoccupied with "How well am I doing?" You are finding yourself when you lose yourself and worry less about who you are. A sinner forgiven, a sufferer sheltered, a saint in process—your welfare is inextricable from our welfare together. We are one in Christ. We are heading home. We will see his face. And all will be made well.[5]

Think about these scared disciples hearing Jesus pray for them and then fast-forward to Acts. The Peter we know in the Gospels is not the Peter we meet in Acts, or even in 1–2 Peter. He's moved from brash and impulsive to humble and pastoral. John falls asleep in the garden when Jesus prays the night before his betrayal, but stands firm all the way to exile on Patmos. The disciples who left Jesus to be handed over to the Jews, gave up their lives for him later. Why? Because Jesus prayed for them and kept them by his Spirit. What he prayed for in John 17 came to pass because his intercession always holds up.

Set-Apart Living

Belief has an object and belief has an effect. We aren't protected so we can stay hidden, and we aren't sanctified so we can keep our holiness to ourselves. The disciples will look different from the world. For them, the world often included Jewish brothers and sisters. They were about to significantly break rank from what they had known and be different both from their religious community and their worldly community.

The way the world sees Christ is by looking at his people, the ones he dwells within. Paul calls us the "aroma of Christ" (2 Cor. 2:15–16 ESV). We look and smell like those set apart from the world. For the disciples, this meant linking arms with people they had nothing in common with. It meant Jews worshipping alongside Gentiles. It meant former, lawless idol worshippers eating in the homes of believing Jews who strongly revered the Law. It means Samaritans and pagans calling Jewish men and women "brothers and sisters."

The entire book of Acts tells the story of the answer to this prayer. Some hate the disciples, some give up everything to follow the Jesus they proclaim. Their lives look different, as they live in the world, but are not of the world. Jesus sends them into the world to continue his rescue mission to redeem a people for himself.

The prayer he prays is the prayer the Father answers.

He Prays for Us

We are the answer to his prayer for the disciples in verses 6–19. Lest we think his prayer is just for his scared disciples, Jesus has the Great Commission in view. In John 17:20–26, he shifts from the immediate to the future, from the disciples of that day to the disciples of the coming ages. "I am praying not only for these disciples," he says to the Father, "but also for all who will ever believe in me through their message" (John 17:20 NLT). In his final moments before the cross, Jesus knows this small Christian movement is going to spread. In fact, that's been his goal all along. Consider Jesus's last words before his ascension in Matthew 28:18–20:

> Jesus came near and said to them, "All authority has been given to me in heaven and on earth. Go, therefore, and make disciples of all nations, baptizing them in the name of the Father and of the Son and of the Holy Spirit, teaching them to observe everything I have commanded you. And remember, I am with you always, to the end of the age."

Again, Jesus is not just praying for his disciples, he's praying for all future believers who come after them. He's praying for us—for you and for me. The pattern of the New Testament church is that they pass it on. The book of Acts is (what my friend, Jen Wilkin says) a "birth narrative."[6] Jesus's death, resurrection, and ascension ushered in a new era—the church of Jesus Christ is born. When Jesus prays for his disciples, he's praying for their efforts in this launch, but in John 17:20–26 he turns toward us, the children of this new family.

So, in the final moments of his earthly life, what exactly are his prayers for us? What does he think is most important for the Father to give us? He prays for three things:

1. Unity
2. Witness
3. Presence

Unity

Jesus prays these words for us in John 17:21–23 (ESV). How many times do you see the word *one*?

> ". . . that they may all be one, just as you, Father, are in me, and I in you, that they also may be in us, so that the world may believe that you have sent me. The glory that you have given me I have given to them, that they may be one even as we are one, I in them and you in me, that they may become perfectly one, so that the world may know that you sent me and loved them even as you loved me."

Unity is a buzzword among Christians. When churches have conflict, we cry for unity. When Christians fight over politics, we push toward unity. Jesus knew it would be hard for us to be united. I think this is why he makes it a prayer point in his last words before his death. It's that important. He doesn't just tell us to be united, he gives us a picture of that unity. Our unity with one another should mirror the unity of the Father and the Son. It's not merely a friendship or closeness, but an unbreaking relationship sealed by the eternal relationship our unity is modeled after. But the unity has a purpose. We don't unite around an idea or a person just to say we have unity. Jesus wants his people to be visible to a watching world. In the same way that our belief has an object and an effect, so does our unity.

Matt Carter and Josh Wredberg say that our unity centers around the gospel. We have a shared belief about who Jesus is and what he came to accomplish. We have a shared unity about God and his purposes in the world. They write,

> The nature of the church's unity is the unity modeled and enabled by the triune God. Just as the

> Father and Son are distinguishable yet perfected unified, so we though different, with different gifts and backgrounds, preferences and appearances, are perfectly united *in* and *through* Christ. If there is a river of love that has eternally flowed between the members of the Trinity, then we find our unity with one another by immersing ourselves completely in it. We get so close to Jesus we become drenched with his love, with the result we cannot help but love one another.[7]

This goes back to what Jesus says in John 15.

Unity is only possible with abiding. It can't be manufactured. It is a supernatural work of God. In fact, it's entirely unnatural to us. The unity Jesus is calling us to is where Jews go to church with Gentiles, which might seem normal to us, but was anathema to the original audience. The entire book of Romans was written to show how Jews and Gentiles could worship together as one body, united by Christ. The early church struggled with unity around Jesus Christ. In Acts 15, the Jerusalem Council gathers to discuss the inclusion of Gentiles into the fold without requiring circumcision. In Philippians, Paul urges the Philippian church toward unity (Phil. 2:2–4), even encouraging two women (by name!) to get along (Phil. 4:2–3). But the basis for our unity is that we're united to Christ, and Christ is united to the Father and the Holy Spirit. As they are completely united to each other, we are completely united to them. And our unity flows out to those who are equally united to them.

But it's hard, isn't it? I'm not Jewish and I don't even know if I worship alongside any ethnic Jews on Sunday morning. And let's be honest, that's not strange to us anymore. The gospel has so spread, that ethnic Jews and Gentiles (anyone who is not Jewish) freely worship together. That prayer has been answered. But we have other barriers to unity, don't we?

In America, and particularly the South (where I live), racial segregation on a Sunday morning is common. It's not because it's a law, but years of systemic injustice, prejudice, and cultural differences have kept us from crossing barriers in worship. We have some dear friends who minister in a black church in our city, and when the husband had his anniversary service, we attended to support him. We were one of a few white families there, but the bigger difference was in the worship style. The same gospel was preached, the same Word was taught, but the expression looked and felt different than our own. When we pulled out of the parking lot to go home, one of our sons asked us if black people go to their own churches and white people go to their own. These were his best friends, but he didn't understand why we went to different churches.

I think this is what Jesus is praying about. There is a unity we have in Christ that runs far deeper than our worship preferences, our culture, our personality, our ethnicity, and even our socioeconomic status. We're united to a Middle Eastern man who lived, died, and rose again over two thousand years ago. And he calls the nations to himself.

It doesn't matter what you wear on Sunday, how much money is in your bank account, what sins you've been saved from (and are being saved from), or even whether you vote Republican or Democrat. Jesus prays you would be united to one another as he is united to the Father and the Spirit. D. A. Carson explains it this way,

> All of this is to the end *that they may believe that you have sent me*. As the display of genuine love amongst believers that they are Jesus' disciples (John 13:34–35), so this display of unity is so

> compelling, so un-worldly, that their witness as to who Jesus is becomes explainable only if Jesus truly is the revealer whom the Father has sent.[8]

It's easy to link arms with people who are like you. It's easy to invite people over who share your interests. It's easy to worship alongside people who feel familiar, vote like you, or even live in your neighborhood. What's harder is to do the opposite. And Jesus prays the world sees us do this, and as a result would know that he alone can save.

Witness

I've alluded to this, but our unity is closely tied to our witness. The disciples bore witness to Jesus, and the church was born. We bear witness to Jesus, and the church continues. Jesus prays for their unity for this purpose: "That the world may know you have sent me and have loved them as you have loved me" (John 17:23).

The world is watching us. I have unbelieving family members, and I imagine you do too. Few things make them more confused about Christ than the lack of unity among Christians, or when Christians behave badly. The sexual abuse crisis in our churches, or pastoral infidelity, or bully pastors, or even the compromise they encounter among Christians in their everyday lives, it all tells a false narrative about who God is and what his Son came to accomplish. Carter and Wredberg say that "the church is the visible display of God's goodness to this world,"[9] so when Christians are unrepentant or celebrate sin, we say something about God that is not true.

Jesus prays that this would not be our story.

When you encounter churches, institutions, and Christians who fail to model this rightly, Jesus wants you to remember this prayer. He prays for it because he knows it will be hard. He prays for it because he wants to see it in our lives and in our witness. He prays for it because it's crucial to his work in the world going forward.

Presence

There's nothing like the pain that comes with missing someone and wanting to be where they are. Just ask the wife of any deployed military husband. Or any lovesick college student saying a final goodbye before he and his high school sweetheart part ways toward two different universities. Or any child that has moved far from home for the first time.

In John 17:24, Jesus shows he is not immune to this sort of feeling. He pleads with the Father: "I want those you have given me to be with me where I am, so that they will see my glory." He wants us home with him. In John 14, he tells us he's getting our home ready, but until then he will be in us, assuring us that home is just an exit away (v. 26). He wants God's presence, which radiates love, to be inside them. And the by-product of this indwelling love is that the world would see his love through us (Rom. 5:5).

The Great Commission shows us that this desire on Jesus's part does not end after he dies and resurrects. As the risen Christ ends the commission with that famous promise—"I am with you until the end of the age"—it is clear that his words in John 17 were not simply sentimentality. Nor were they a fretful, temporal, last-ditch effort to stay with his friends instead of going to the cross. No. To be with us, for us to be with him where he is, is an enduring desire of the Savior before the cross and after it, into eternity. It's a promise that begins in the garden and is carried through as the center point of the Scriptures—God desires to dwell among his people.

Of all the things, Jesus could pray for us, he prays for the things that plague us the most in our modern age. That makes me think it's always been a struggle for God's people. We've always preferred our tribes over unity. We've always struggled with our lives matching our witness. And we've always wondered if he really is with us when we can't trace his hand.

What's in It for Me?

If you had just a few moments left with the people you loved, what would you pray for them? As a mom, I know my sons intimately. There are things I pray for them that few know they struggle with, but I do. If I only had moments left with them, I would plead with them about the things I pray for them—the things that last.

Jesus knew his friends, so much better than I know my sons. And he knows us, so much better than we know ourselves. He knows what's coming, so he prays proactively. He's the type of Savior who covers all his bases before he leaves. He's the type of older brother who paves the way for his less mature siblings. He's a Savior to believe in because in a world where people forget us, he prays for us. And his prayers are effective.

We're the ones he prays for, but we're not the ones on the hook for making sure those prayers come to pass. The entire emphasis of this prayer is on Christ's power to finish what he starts. And it begins at the cross.

8

His Presence Restores My Trust

The Weight of Glory and the Caretaker

When my fourth son was a baby, I threw my back out. Pregnancies with little rest in between took its toll. But in addition to the stress my body had undergone, there was also something missing in my daily life. I didn't lift weights. The additional pregnancy weight put pressure on my muscles, and I had no strength to support me (or my spine). Instead of activating my glutes, I activated my back every time I lifted my baby, toddler, or even twin preschoolers. Seven months into having four kids four and under, and my back decided it was done doing all the work.

After a couple of days in bed, I finally made it to the physical therapist. Part of my healing journey included weight-bearing exercises. Every time I went to PT (which was twice a week early on), I had to use weights. And then I was given extra exercises to do at home on the off days. In those early months of physical therapy, I learned that running was not going to cut it. I needed to factor strength training into my post-baby routine. It wasn't my favorite piece of advice. To this day, I hate strength training. I'd choose a cardio workout any day. Leg day never feels good to me. I dread my scheduled weight days. And the endorphin boost I get from running, swimming, or riding the Peloton never comes when I lift weights. I feel only dread.

Though my perspective on weights tends to be negative (or on a good day, maybe *tolerable*), the apostle Paul speaks of weight in positive terms. In 2 Corinthians 4:16–18, he talks about a weight of glory that exceeds anything we possess here, but also exceeds our present trials and suffering. He sees weight as a benefit, one that fits us for heaven and builds up our endurance. In other words, Paul sees the value in leg day. He writes,

> Therefore we do not give up. Even though our outer person is being destroyed, our inner person is being renewed day by day. For our momentary light affliction is producing for us an absolutely incomparable eternal weight of glory. So we do not focus on what is seen, but on what is unseen. For what is seen is temporary, but what is unseen is eternal.

We Saw His Glory (Holly's Story)

Holly understands the value of the weight metaphor better than I do. God took Holly on a journey to experience this weight of glory. Initially, she didn't enjoy the extra weight. But over time, Paul's words became dear to her.

When Holly was thirty-four weeks pregnant with her third child, her husband was diagnosed with the most advanced form of lymphatic cancer. She prided herself on her strength, but now she had no strength. She prided herself in her ability to do things right, to be the good "Christian" girl. But she couldn't do enough good things to save her husband. The weight of this suffering pressed in on her. The weight of glory countered by the weight of bad news, and she felt helpless on every front. The prospect of being a single mom to her young children, and unborn baby, overwhelmed her. She couldn't "obey" enough to get herself out of this circumstance.

We met over coffee one spring morning, and she told me about her journey coming to terms with the weight of glory.

> Even though I had grown up in church and graduated from a Christian university, I had only been really growing in Christ for about a year and a half [when my husband got sick]. I was studying the Gospel of John with other women in my community, and we were learning about his journey to the cross. Recognizing that my keeping all the Christian to-do's and avoiding the don'ts had NOT saved me, I was, for the first time growing in an awareness of my own depravity and utter dependence on Jesus. Then this news hit our family like a ceiling crashing on us. I knew how his journey to the cross would end with Jesus walking out of an empty tomb, fully alive and having defeated death by absorbing God's holy and perfect wrath on behalf of sinners like me—and my godly young husband. And because of Jesus's priestly prayer in John 17 and God's faithful comforter, his Holy Spirit, two days after this diagnosis I realized that even though I didn't know how Sandy's journey would end in coming months or years, I knew that we—our little family—would be kept by our loving and gracious and merciful Father.

In the coming months, Holly witnessed God's sustaining power in her life, even when all signs pointed to her emotional and spiritual demise. God restored her trust, and showed her that he was someone to believe in. We often hear stories of church being a source of pain for people, but for Holly, gathering with God's people became the means of carrying her through these dark days. On a Friday she felt the weight of it all. She had a five-year-old and a two-year-old. Her husband had Stage 4 cancer and her father was also recently sick, leaving her without family support. She was also very pregnant. Having recently studied the Gospel of John, all she could remember was the words of Jesus, "I have kept them." But the weight of the suffering was too much, and didn't feel like "keeping." It took the weight of her suffering for her to see the weight of glory God had for her. She felt like Moses in the wilderness, when God said he would hide Moses in the rock, but let his goodness and name pass by him. She got a glimpse of his goodness.

> That day was a Sunday. My five-year-old and I stood surrounded by other messy people experiencing tragedy, uncertainty, and joy. We were singing an old Gaither hymn, and I knew: I could face tomorrow; I could experience freedom from fear; I could find life worth living, all because he lives. Standing there with other believers, holding my child's hand, singing "Because He Lives," I felt the weight of glory. Studying John brought depth and richness to these lyrics that ministered to my anxious heart and set me on a journey of trusting the Lord for his daily grace, protection, and provision. We had studied John, and particularly John 17, where Jesus says, "I have kept them." He loves them to the end (John 16). In the midst of all of it he gives them another command, "love one another." That's how he was showing his glory to this little family. We couldn't count on family. My

> dad was sick. My husband was sick. But my church family showed us Jesus keeps us. He showed his glory to us through people.
>
> We saw his glory through people.

Before her husband's cancer, Holly saw her life in terms of what she could and couldn't do. She trusted in her own strength. But in everything being stripped from her, she saw that she can't control anything. She can't do enough. It's about God's keeping power.

As she reflected on Jesus's words in John 17, knowing that Jesus was choosing a hard path to do what we could not do for ourselves, it made her fearful that he would require a hard path for her. And he did. But her fear of being alone on the hard path never materialized. Remembering Jesus's prayer in John 17, his care in spite of his agony, both spiritual and physical restored her trust that he sees, knows, and cares.

> It was hard to believe that he really cared about the details of my days. He is trustworthy even when I can't see, or know, and when I care more about myself than anything. He understands my humanity.

And in those early days of her husband's diagnosis, she felt her humanity. She felt helpless and out of control. But God used the gathered church, meeting her needs and worshipping alongside her, to make the "weight" training worth it. The weight was heavy, but it yielded results. It was a net positive, even when the weights felt too heavy. It led to trust, which led to endurance, which led to greater faith.

I'm happy to report that her husband is now cancer free. So is her father. Holly gave birth to her third child, and they were able to raise them together, always remembering the reminder that "because he lives I can face tomorrow." He's loved them to the end.

Faith in Caretaking (Christa's Story)

Caretaking is a thankless job. For a mother caring for small children, there are websites and ministries devoted to encouraging moms along their journey. But for the person caring for an elderly parent or grandparent, it is isolating. Christa shares how caring for her grandmother led her to doubt God's care for her and ultimately restore her faith in him. When we tell stories of people who persevere, it's helpful to see that the journey toward endurance is as important as the result. It's helpful to hear it in her own words.

> I took care of my grandmother for ten years. Toward the end of that time, it became so difficult that I didn't think I could do it any longer. I had lost weight, was going through early menopause, my marriage was struggling, and anxiety had taken over, not just mentally but physically. For the first time in many years, I did not want to obey and endure my current circumstances. I wanted freedom to live how I wanted to live for God, but apart from my situation. My grandmother, who raised me and was my biggest supporter my entire life, was now critical and mean. She was very hostile and judgmental. She was unhappy with everything I tried to do for her and angry continually. It was a difficult environment emotionally, and as my body began to worsen with stress-induced symptoms, I felt I could no longer be still and trust him. I felt like I had to save myself from the

situation and remove myself as her caregiver, or I would continue to decline as well. It was hard to trust him because I didn't see a gentle way out, and I felt I had tried everything I could. The Lord gave me the word *endurance*, and I did NOT want to hear that!

I didn't think I could "do it" any longer. Instead, I fought for my own freedom. Instead of enduring until the very end, I fought against the Lord and my loved ones. I felt so alone and even felt God had given up on me because of my giving up on myself and how HE could sustain me.

I think the hardest thing for me during that time in trusting the Lord was the effect caregiving had on my physical, mental, and spiritual health. As my grandmother's health continued to decline, her attitude toward me declined as well. She had been the one person in my life who had loved and cared for me, even raised me. She was my constant supporter until she wasn't . . . anymore.

When the day came for us to head to assisted living and settle her in, she had forgotten that we had an appointment to be there and take her things with us. I was at the end of my rope (I thought), and I was demanding and angry now. We left her home in a way that I will always regret. I wish I had trusted him "just a little bit longer" so the exit could have been a more peaceful one.

After all was said and done, my grandmother went to a long-term care facility and we put the house up for sale. I felt defeated. I felt alone and unsupported. I felt completely misunderstood. I was so discouraged and full of doubt. I felt like a failure. I was tired and felt depressed. One day, before leaving, God spoke to me while I was standing in my bedroom, alone. He said, "Without a vision, the people perish." I knew it was him. I went and grabbed my Bible and opened it. There, on the page, was Proverbs 29:18. The exact Scripture he just dropped into my spirit. I asked him, "What does perish actually mean there, Lord?" I looked up the original Hebrew word and it means "To let go, to loose" (on a basic level "to come to nothing"). He showed me that in order have a victorious life on the other side of it all, I had to get a vision for my future, for our future. I was SO EXCITED because when he spoke to me, I knew I had purpose again beyond my current circumstances. God restored (slowly, over time) our marriage, my identity in Christ, and my outlook on life.

Jesus restored my trust in him by showing me later that no matter how you feel at any moment, if you rush his timing, you will have some regrets. The Word tells us that we can do all things through Christ who gives us strength (Phil. 4:13). I see now that I could have endured by trusting his timing without having a meltdown! I felt I had to fight my way out. I know now that was just my body and mind reacting to continued stress, and the next time a stressful situation comes around, I can endure it with God's peace instead of fighting his timing.

Sometimes, God wraps up our suffering with a tidy bow. Sometimes, we end with regret for our response throughout the suffering. The beauty of Christ's work is that he is the same both in our past and in our present. His grace is sufficient for our past failures and our present struggles. He is the Good Shepherd who never leaves his sheep. He is a faithful friend, who stays with us to the end. He is with us in our suffering, sustaining us by his indwelling presence through the Holy Spirit. He is praying for us right now, asking God to keep us faithful all the way to the end. And it's to this end that we turn in our final section.

PART 3

THE SAME IN THE FUTURE

9

He Will Provide for You

(John 6)

I HAVEN'T HAD A newborn in years, but sometimes I wake up in the middle of the night to the phantom sound of an infant's cry. *The body keeps the score*, especially when you spent consecutive sleepless nights feeding and consoling a hungry baby. That 2:00 a.m. wail for food doesn't leave your brain without a fight.

When a baby feels hunger, he has one thing on his mind—eating. An adult presses through hunger pains, knowing that another meal is on its way. But a baby, he's not mature enough to trust that the person who fed him three hours ago will be there again with a warmed bottle within minutes of his first cry. And every new parent knows, the thankless effort is only made bearable by the helplessness of your precious baby. He can't thank you. He can't talk to you. He can only demand from you. He wants you for what you give him. He cries for food every time he feels the urge to eat, and he cries like the next meal is nowhere to be found—even when you're standing groggily over his crib.

The path to maturity is realizing that the hand that feeds you is the hand that keeps you every step of your development journey.

The same is true for the Christian life. There's a reason God uses metaphors like the one in 1 Peter, where he tells his readers to long for God's word like a baby for warm milk (1 Pet. 2:2). Jesus knows we don't outgrow the hunger cues we're born with. We reapply them to other areas of our lives, wondering if the same God who fed us as infants through the efforts of our parents will also feed us and keep us all the way to the end.

It's hard to think when you're hungry. It's hard to trust too.

In John 6, we come upon some hungry people. Like a baby who can't see the bottle waiting in the bottle warmer, the disciples can't see how the food in front of them will satisfy everyone. And Jesus takes the slow journey from feeding hungry bellies to helping them see that the hand that feeds them is the hand that keeps them.

As we've been exploring in this book, people have their reasons for walking away from Jesus. Sometimes people face suffering and can't see how Jesus will carry them through the pain. Sometimes people think the approach of doing some good on its own is enough to save them—who needs Jesus and the church? Sometimes people are hurt by the church or leaders in the church, and they can't separate the Good Shepherd from the under-shepherds (or the sheep).

But there is a lack of belief that stems from hunger. There is an unbelief whose origin is from the desire to fill the famished belly. When the pains are too great, you reach for the Cheetos instead of waiting for the steak, vegetable, and potato. Instead of waiting for the life-sustaining meal, you take the snack that gives a blood sugar boost, only to crash soon after.

And once you doubt he can provide your next meal, you doubt he can keep you fed for the rest of your life. So, you settle for Cheetos and accept your synthetic carb-induced demise.

That's a little dramatic, but you get the point.

When we meet the disciples at the beginning of John 6, Jesus tests them to see if they'll settle for his meal versus the quick fix that running to the store brings. He uses the blessing of a miraculous feeding to reveal where true nourishment can be found. In using physical bread as a metaphor for spiritual nourishment, he warns against trusting in the bread only. It's not wrong to pray for physical food, it's just wrong to worship it. On the flip side, Christ wants us to worship him as the true bread, not for the physical bread and blessings he provides.

A Test of Faith

Often in John, Jesus performs a sign to prove his claims about himself. Here he performs a sign—multiplying bread and fish—to prove a deeper reality about his identity.

But he also points back to the defining moment in their history—Moses leading God's people in the wilderness. There is a key contextual clue included in John 6 that helps us see what this miracle triggered in the mind of the disciples. In John 6:4, John tells us that the "Passover was near." All of this happens around Passover, so their senses are heightened to the metaphor. In the Passover, God's people were delivered from death before they were delivered from Pharoah. Every year, they were reminded of their escape from Egypt. Every year, they were reminded that salvation came from another in their place. For hundreds of years, they kept this going, and it always pointed them back to God's provision during their bondage in Egypt. It pointed them to the hand that fed them, but also the hand that kept them alive through many dangers, toils, and snares.

If you follow their story in Exodus, you know they didn't just escape from Egypt into the promised land. They wandered in the desert for forty years. During their wandering, God provided food from heaven for them every single day. They never starved, but they went to their tents to sleep every night wondering if the same manna they found that morning would be there when they woke again the next day. And it was. For forty years, God never left them hungry.

The Jewish people were wrapped up in this story. They ate unleavened bread at Passover, reminding them of their hasty exit from Egypt. They held festivals and feasts to commemorate their shared deliverance and continued trust that the same God who kept them in the wilderness, kept them still while they waited for a greater deliverance.

But the struggle for them is real. While they can look back on a long history of God showing up for them, they can also look back on a long history of their repeated doubts that he can and did. They doubted the hand that fed them, and then doubted he would keep them.

This is why Jesus uses this metaphor here—at this time and in this place in John 6. The natural fallen impulse is to doubt God's provision. In the wilderness, their grumbling against the manna came while the manna was still in their hands—sometimes as they were gathering the day's food, they doubted it would come again tomorrow. Sometimes while they ate this miraculous provision in a barren land, they wished for something better. Yet, every day, God sent more. Every day, he provided for them. Every day, God sent bread from heaven to satisfy their hunger. They never lacked, even when they wandered in the desert (when they should have had no access to food and water), they were kept by a daily blessing of food. Here in John 6, the question of bread and food and the sign Jesus performs should trigger their minds to remember this core memory for the people. The story that had been passed down for ages from their parents and grandparents was being lived out in front of them.

The conversation between Andrew, Philip, and Jesus is one we see frequently in the Gospels. An impossible situation is met with a powerful solution through the Savior. Philip and Andrew hear Jesus tell the crowd of people to sit down and watch him call the young boy over with his loaves and fishes. Thousands have been following Jesus, and now they are all hungry—but no one knows where they will get enough food to feed everyone. They see the raw materials in front of them (five loaves and two fish), but both Andrew and Philip question how Jesus will provide food for all these people. At a minimum, there were five thousand men there, which means the total number is more like twenty thousand if you count the women and children in tow. Philip essentially says, "there's no place to buy enough bread." Andrew takes it a step farther and questions whether the boy's bread could ever be enough for all these people (vv. 7–8). He's not wrong. Food doesn't multiply, especially in first-century Israel. Finding more food took a significant effort, sometimes an entire day. It was hard enough to feed the small group of disciples, so Philip and Andrew can't wrap their minds around how Jesus will feed the crowd too.

But they failed the test. They looked at the raw materials (a little bread and fish for a whole lot of people) and concluded feeding them wasn't possible—even when the man they'd seen work miracles was the one asking them what to do next. Like the Israelites in the wilderness, Philip and Andrew only see what's in front of them. They don't see *the One* in front of them for who he is and what he came to do.

The Christian life is, among many things, a battle to believe that God will meet your needs. Like a baby wailing for his next bottle, we forget that he's never missed a meal. We doubt. We scream. We stress over the outcome.

We need examples we can feel, taste, and touch. As much as we want it to be enough to know in our minds that daily bread comes from heaven, our stomachs betray us after a few hours.

What I love about this story is that Jesus doesn't just give them enough food to settle the hunger pains. He gives them as much as they wanted (v. 11). No one lacks. No one must ask for more. No one must feel hunger pains when they leave to head home. You would think this is enough for every person present to fall on their faces in worship. The purpose of the Gospel of John, remember, is belief. These stories are written down for us to read them and believe that Jesus is the Christ (John 20:31). But belief doesn't work that way. In fact, sometimes the provision has the opposite effect. It makes us content, until we feel the need again and run back for more. Sometimes the provision in one area makes us realize how much we lack in another. That's what happened with the crowd in John 6.

As I mentioned previously, there were likely over twenty thousand people on that grassy knoll eating their fill of bread and fish. Perhaps they didn't all know where it came from as they passed the overflowing baskets around. They just ate. But word traveled, and by the time everyone is stuffed to capacity, they are ready to make Jesus king (v. 15). R. C. Sproul comments that the Jewish people were under the thumb of Roman rule at this time. They were desperate for relief, and their hopes were set on the Messiah coming to deliver them from Roman oppression and establish his kingdom right then. When Jesus miraculously feeds them during Passover, their hope is quickened to expect this immediate deliverance. But a temporal king with sights set merely on Rome is not the kind of king they need—nor is it the kind of kingdom Jesus came to establish.[1]

The satiated hunger made them want more—it made them want the comfort of a kingdom right then. It made them never want to feel discomfort again. It made them rush for a remedy to make their life easy. And Jesus would have none of that. He's on a mission to save and keep his people, but not in the way they always want or expect.

He wants us to want *him*, not merely the bread he provides.

Don't Trust the Bread

Jesus withdraws like he does every time he perceives the people misunderstand his purpose. When he re-emerges on the other side of the sea (after performing an equally miraculous sign of walking on water), the people are waiting for him. He knows they're looking for another sign because of what he says to them:

> "Truly I tell you, you are looking for me, not because you saw the signs, but because you ate the loaves and were filled. Don't work for the food that perishes but for the food that lasts for eternal life, which the Son of Man will give you, because God the Father has set his seal of approval on him." (John 6:26–27)

In John 6, Jesus gives them bread, but then tells them to lift their gaze away from the temporal to the eternal. In other words, *don't trust the bread*. Word traveled fast that Jesus multiplied the loaves and fish, so by the time Jesus arrives across the sea from Capernaum, the crowd awaits him. When Jesus arrives, he offers a stern warning, saying, "Don't look for me just because I gave you your fill of temporary bread and now you want more. Look for me because I'll give you the sort of food that lasts forever."

The crowd succumbs to the natural human impulse—follow the hand that feeds you.

One of my favorite children's books to read with my kids is *Bear Wants More*. The book follows Bear, who never seems to have enough to eat. He eats and eats, and still wants more. Every page leads him on a journey for more food, until he ends the book collapsed in hibernation. The people are like Bear. They've eaten the bread Jesus gave them, and they want more. Like the Israelites in the wilderness, today's manna wasn't enough. They want to see what tomorrow holds too.

Jesus knows this about the human condition, so he urges them to look past the temporal. They understand that Moses and Jesus gave them food, but they don't understand that the one greater than Moses is here. Moses simply pointed the people to the One who gave them manna every day in the wilderness. Jesus is the One who comes from heaven to give them himself (vv. 32–35).

This discourse between them leads Jesus to make another "I AM" statement. This time he says, "I am the bread of life" (v. 35). They come to Jesus hungry and leave with him saying, "If you come to me, you'll never be hungry again."

Right now, I'm hungry. It's mid-morning and I'm too far removed from breakfast. Is Jesus's saying not true for me because my stomach growls and I haven't grabbed my snack yet? What about Christians living in poverty and dying of starvation? The threat of unbelief looms heavy over this statement if we take Jesus's words literally. Christian history and current events are littered with faithful believers living with hunger pains. Jesus Christ is our provision of bread in the wilderness, but life in a broken world means sometimes his people still starve.

He's getting at something deeper. The path toward belief means we need to understand the difference between his words and our reality. If we misunderstand him, we can wind up like the Israelites, grumbling in the wilderness looking for more. Like his conversation with the Samaritan woman in John 4, our hunger and need to be filled reveals a spiritual need that only he can meet. He's using the physical reality to point to the spiritual need.

The Samaritan woman satisfied her craving for protection and love by following all the typical tactics and found in Jesus a well that never runs dry. The Jewish people in John 6 (and if we're honest, us too) are filling their hungry bellies with Cheetos, when they really need the bread of life to sustain them. Jesus tells them how he feeds them in verses 53–56 (and it sounds a little crazy),

> "Unless you eat the flesh of the Son of Man and drink his blood, you do not have life in yourselves. The one who eats my flesh and drinks my blood has eternal life, and I will raise him up on the last day, because my flesh is true food and my blood is true drink. The one who eats my flesh and drinks my blood remains in me, and I in him."

These are themes he carries throughout the Gospel of John, but in this discourse, it's centered around food and drink. The way you are sustained is through belief in him. The way you believe in him is by finding all your spiritual nourishment in him alone. And because they aren't feeding on him (believing in him), they think his bread isn't enough because they are burning through their temporal quick fixes to satiate their deep spiritual hunger. They want more because they're trusting the bread, not the Bread of Life.

Every meal comes from the hand of God. It's why we pray before we eat. We thank God for the blessing of food. But when we are hungry, or when we lack something we want, how do we respond? Do we pray? Are we desperate? Do we look to the Giver? Or are we like the crowd, reverting back to all the world's strategies of getting what it wants because we're captive to our desires? One commentator writes,

> We often hunger for the wrong bread. Why do you think the people got in boats and traveled across the sea to find Jesus (vv. 2–25)? Was it because they understood he was the one who could quench their spiritual hunger, he was the one who could fill the emptiness inside their souls? Jesus said they

> were seeking him because they wanted more bread to eat (v. 26). One author said, "They were moved not by full hearts, but by full bellies" (Morris, *John*, 358).[2]

The physical hunger we all feel is a metaphor for the spiritual hunger we all have. When we lack, it should lead to greater dependence. When we have, it should lead to greater trust.

Jesus tells them not to work for the food that perishes. I live in Arkansas, which means that in summer humidity lays on us like a thick blanket. It's swampy, hot, and you sweat the minute you step outside. It also means that food doesn't last long. Bananas go bad within days. Bread grows mold overnight. Physical food can't be kept. Earthly provision can't either. I don't have food insecurity, so my temptation to trust the bread like the Israelites is nonexistent. But I have other "bread" that I put my trust in. I spent the last twenty years working toward a seminary degree so I could serve on staff in a church. Once I had the church job of my dreams, I thought I had "made it." There was nothing else I wanted to do. But then I didn't have it any longer, and I spent the better part of a year trying to discern what was next.

Who am I when the work is gone? Who am I when I don't have what I've prayed for anymore? How do I trust when the only thing I've ever wanted to do is taken away?

These are questions I've had to wrestle through. Do I come to Jesus Christ for the provision, or do I come to him for life? Is he enough to provide for me, even when I walk away "empty handed" of earthly provision? I walk into a new church with an empty belly every Sunday and, like Andrew and Philip, wonder where the next meal will come from. It's in the lack where belief is the hardest to locate.

The Hand That Feeds Is the Hand That Keeps

In the wilderness, God's people weren't given bread for tomorrow. All they had was today's manna. And every night, they went to bed hoping it would arrive with the sunrise. Every day it was waiting for them when they stepped outside the tent. We all have wilderness seasons, where we lay our head on the pillow and pray for belief that the bread he promises for tomorrow will be there when we need it. And pray that today's manna lasts us until sundown.

For me, every Sunday I'm pulled back into belief—is the bread of life enough for this moment? Will the manna I eat this morning be enough for this Sunday? I can't carry tomorrow's hope into today. I need today's bread. He meets me there, and I do it all again next week. The challenge for the wilderness season is to believe that the bread he provides is enough, even when we can't see where it will come from or what time it will arrive. The challenge to belief is thinking God won't provide for us right now, and forever. We doubt provision in the moment, but we also take that doubt to its logical conclusion and wonder if he will take us all the way home. Like the crowd, we hold out for more miracles because the one he performed yesterday isn't enough. Like Bear, we want more.

John 6 is a siren call of belief to the doubter who thinks God won't feed you. It's a challenge to not trust the hunger pains. Don't trust the lack, trust the true Bread who never runs out. Throughout this text, there are markers pointing to an abundance of care. John tells us not only that they got as much food as they wanted, but also that they ate until they were full (v. 12). This crowd passed around the baskets until they couldn't eat another piece of bread or fish. And then there were leftovers. Imagine, they came hungry, and left with to-go boxes. When Jesus tells them, "I am the bread of life. Feast on me and you'll never be hungry again," he was saying this to a satisfied crowd.

This was better than what Israel had in the wilderness. In the wilderness, they didn't believe he would provide, but when he did, he exceeded their desires. They lacked nothing—for forty years. Every day, God faithfully showed up. How could they not trust him every year after? But they didn't have leftovers each day. They only had that day's bread, and they laid their head on the pillow each night trusting that tomorrow they would wake up with more food.

If you have ever faced lack (whether it's food insecurity, financial need, or something else), you know how hard it is to trust God when you don't know when the next helping will come. Jesus tells this crowd, someone better than Moses is here. In him, they always know where the next meal comes from. The impulse that kept them from trusting in the wilderness was unbelief. And in their unbelief, they complained and doubted God's care. They never went without, yet they always thought God was holding out on them. He forced them into a posture of faith every day for those forty years. Often, he does the same with us. He provides in abundance, but then makes us wait for more. He answers one prayer with "yes," and another with "no." It's actually for our good that God protects us from abundance (Prov. 30:8–9). Having too much wealth, food, or resources leads us to a life of complacency both in our walk with God and our posture toward others. It's why God urged Israel in the wilderness to not forget God even when they moved into the promised land. Riches lull us into a false sense of security. He knows this about us, so he gives us boundary lines. When we wait on him to provide, we're tempted to doubt he cares. When we are overflowing in abundance, we're tempted to remember that he's the giver of all good things.

In the waiting, unbelief threatens us. But like the Israelites in the wilderness, and the crowd on the hill, we've been given more than we can ask for. As Paul says in Romans 8:31–32,

> If God is for us, who is against us? He did not even spare his own Son but gave him up for us all. How will he not also with him grant us everything?

Jesus gives them an appetizer of the coming feast when he says that the bread he gives is his very life. The way they are sustained is through the life he gives them, but he has to die first. When we doubt his provision in the moment, we remember there's nothing more he can give. He gave us his very life to feast on forever. If that reality is true, and it is, then certainly we can trust him whatever temporary morsels we need in this life.

This Bread Is Built to Last

Jesus is masterful at using signs to magnify his identity and glory. In this section, the sign of multiplying loaves and fishes (which interestingly comes up in every Gospel, but is applied differently each time), points back to the manna in the wilderness. But it sets the crowd up for this profound statement from Jesus: "I am the bread of life." He is the bread that comes down from heaven. He is the bread that sustains the people forever. He is the bread that satiates so they don't have to keep looking for food that perishes. Our temptation toward doubting his provision is often because we trust the wrong bread. We trust the bread that gets moldy after a few days, when the bread that lasts holds out his hand to us. The crowd came to him for more because they wanted more of the bread from yesterday. They wanted full bellies. We do the same when we turn from him whenever we feel hunger pains.

Jesus mentions the word *bread* fourteen times in this discourse. That's not counting his references to manna and eating. And then issues a remarkable charge:

> "I am the bread of life. Your ancestors ate the manna in the wilderness, and they died. This is the bread that comes down from heaven so that anyone may eat of it and not die. I am the living bread that came down from heaven. If anyone eats this bread he will live forever. The bread that I will give for the life of the world is my flesh." (vv. 48–51)

Moses gave them bread that needed to be gathered daily. It didn't last. It was never meant to sustain them forever because it was designed to point them beyond the moment. When Jesus comes on the scene and says, "I am the bread of life," he's making the claim that one greater than Moses is here. Moses told them *about* the bread—how to get it, how often it would descend, where it would come from—but Jesus *is* the bread.

To our modern ears, this all sounds a little strange. We don't eat people, especially if we want to be nourished. Cannibalism is a universally unacceptable practice among civilized nations. And the crowd seems to understand this as well asking, "How can this man give us his flesh to eat?"

The key to understanding what Jesus is saying is found in the verse that comes right before these. In verse 47 he sets them up for understanding what he means by "eating" his flesh and "drinking" his blood. "Truly I tell you, anyone who believes has eternal life."

It's the same word we've been coming back to all throughout this book—belief. Jesus is not endorsing cannibalism. He's calling us to find our satisfaction in him alone. He's urging us to believe that he is enough. That so much more than manna, *he* is the all-satisfying thing the Father sent down to earth to fill us with. Don't be like the ancestors in the wilderness, who put all their hope in daily bread that perishes. The relief to your hunger pains is found in being fed by the Savior. He's the well that never runs dry and the bread that fills you up and nourishes you completely. He wants them, and us, to believe that Messiah has come. Jesus seems to even know they would be confused by this, so he says, "the bread that I will give for the life of the world is my flesh" (v. 51). By the end of the Gospel, he will have done just that.

The ancestors grumbled in the wilderness. They thought only in the temporal. They wanted more than what God provided them. They had full bellies and began to trust the bread, not the hand that fed them. But it led to them always feeling discontent. They never got over their grumbling for something better.

The people in this scene are no different. They aren't running after Jesus because they want him. They're running after him because they want what he can give them. And we see this in their response to him. In effect, Jesus tells them, "You won't live unless you drink my blood and eat my flesh. Meaning, you won't be satisfied unless you're united to *me*, as I am united to my Father. You won't make it if you don't receive *me*, the true bread of life."

> "This teaching is hard. Who can accept it?" (v. 60)

That's their response. And John tells us from that point on, many of his disciples moved on because they couldn't accept his call on their life.

They wanted the stuff he provided, but they didn't want him. In a moment of weakness, their hunger led them to cry out to him. But when their bellies were full, they looked for something more than run-of-the-mill belief in the Son of God. They wanted the quick fix of Cheetos, but not the sustaining power of the Bread of Life.

The Outcome

Jesus is undeterred by this. In the wilderness, and in the beginning of John 6, physical hunger reigns supreme. Even in our own lives, when we lack something—whether it's food or something else—it's all we think about. Our physical hunger matters, but it is intended to point to a deeper spiritual hunger we all possess, but often fail to recognize.

In the wilderness, the physical hunger they felt every day reminded them that they needed to depend on God to meet their daily needs. What about our own spiritual hunger? When we wrestle with doubts and God doesn't answer right away, it leads us to wonder if the hand that feeds is the hand that keeps us. But listen to his words in John 6:35–39:

> "No one who comes to me will ever be hungry, and no one who believes in me will ever be thirsty again. . . . Everyone the Father gives me will come to me, and the one who comes to me I will never cast out. For I have come down from heaven, not to do my own will, but the will of him who sent me. This is the will of him who sent me: that I should lose none of those he has given me but should raise them up on the last day."

Jesus had one purpose when he came to earth: to bring his wayward people back to him. He offers his life up as our continual food—we live because he died. His body broken for us forever satisfies all our spiritual longings. And there isn't a single mouth he misses when he offers his life as our spiritual food.

He doesn't lose a single one.

The message of John 6 is that if he meticulously feeds his people every day of our wilderness journey, he won't let us starve in the final day. He leaves no meal half cooked. And there is more than enough to go around.

But you must believe. You must take him at his word and on his terms. You must want him more than you want the temporary morsels he provides. This is what I've had to accept even as I'm stripped of the one thing I've wanted in my adult life. I must believe he's enough, even when I don't know what tomorrow holds.

Many hear Jesus's words and decide it's too much for them, so they jump ship. Jesus looks at Peter and asks if he wants to do the same, and Peter gives this great line of belief—"Lord, to whom will we go? You have the words of eternal life. We have come to believe and know that you are the Holy One of God" (vv. 68–69).

Peter gets in trouble for his tongue a lot in the Gospels, but his greatest weakness is also his greatest strength. When he speaks on impulse, sometimes its cringeworthy and sometimes it's gold. This is a golden moment. Peter looks at the costs to feasting on the Bread of Life and concludes that this is the best option. The alternatives will always leave them wanting more. No matter what awaits him, he makes this bold confession of belief.

All throughout John 6, the disciples struggle with Jesus's actions and his words. They don't see how he can work a miracle. They ask him for something better than the sign he just performed. They ask what works they need to do to be accepted by him. They doubt that he is enough. They grumble when he tells them they can't do anything, but he is the one who will do it all for them. They misunderstand his purpose and misinterpret his statements.

It's hard to accept that there is nothing we bring to our salvation. It's hard to accept that the call to follow Jesus means we suffer with him. It's hard to accept that Jesus is enough to satiate your hunger pains, especially when you're still waiting on daily bread.

But after hearing him speak of his provision in the wilderness, how can we not gladly feast on him always? Nothing else will satisfy. Nothing will satiate the hunger pains. Nothing will keep us full all the way to the end. We come to him for more because we want more of him, not because he gives us empty calories and we need a blood sugar boost. We come to him empty and walk away full of a better provision than earthly food that we burn through by lunch time.

He is the hand that feeds us, but he's also the hand that keeps us. As we feast on him, he won't lose a single one. He is someone to believe in because where all other means of earthly satisfaction fail, he will satisfy our hunger pains all the way to the feast in glory.

10

He Will End All Suffering

John 11

The clock turned just past midnight and my ears strained to hear my toddler's cries. I looked at my husband, contemplated my next move, and promptly turned over in the bed. His cries for "Momma" were clear over the sound machine and walls between us, but sleep won out. I heard his cries, but I stayed in my bed. I heard his pleas, but I delayed.

Do I love him?

Before you stop reading, let me assure you, this story is fictional. But as moms, we endure sleepless nights, changes to our bodies, schedules that keep us running carpool all over the city, and so much more to give our kids the best. Our love is shown in running toward them, not away from them—especially when they call for us.

Many would say the highest attribute of God, and particularly God the Son, is his love. We all learned the song "Jesus loves me this I know, for the Bible tells me so." There are attributes people don't love about Jesus, but everyone can get behind the love of Christ.

And in John 11, we're told that Jesus loves Mary, Martha, and their brother Lazarus. The scene begins with Jesus away from his beloved friends. But that doesn't stop them from getting a message to him—"Lord, the one you love is sick." It's so important for us to know Jesus loves them that John mentions it twice at the very beginning of this scene. There is no confusion about Jesus's relationship status with this family. He loves them.

That's why it is so surprising how Jesus responds to their request for him to come. When we meet them in John 11, they're desperate for their brother. Lazarus is sick, so they send for Jesus. And of course they would. As Jesus's friends, they've witnessed his signs. They've seen him heal others, even ones who reject him. They naturally expect Jesus to drop everything and run to the one he loves when Lazarus is on his deathbed. Instead, Jesus's response in John 11:6 (ESV) surprises us: "So, when he heard that Lazarus was ill, he stayed two days longer in the place where he was." Notice it does not say he tried his best to race to Lazarus's side, but unfortunately stumbled upon two days of unforeseen travel delays. It does not say a storm delayed him, nor a more important matter. No. As we'll see, Jesus *intentionally* delays coming for two whole days. These sisters send for their friend to come heal their brother. But Jesus waits.

It's as shocking to us as a mom who ignores the cries of her child in the middle of the night. A mother runs to her children. A Savior runs to the friends he loves. And yet, Jesus doesn't do what's expected. He does the opposite. And in case we suppose it's simply because Jesus doesn't really love this family, take a look at the verse right before John 11:6:

> Now Jesus loved Martha, her sister, and Lazarus. So when he heard that he was sick, he stayed two more days in the place where he was. (vv. 5–6)

Do you see the logic John is building out here? A, so B. Jesus loved these people. So, he waited.

What? Why would he do this?

John gives specific details on the timing because he wants us to focus on the number of days Jesus delayed. He mentions more than once that Jesus waits two days to depart—which ensures that by the time he arrives in Bethany, Lazarus has been buried four days (John 11:17). Jesus knew Lazarus was in critical condition, so he waited. Jesus knew his friends needed him, but he delayed. We're left to infer he let Lazarus die. He knows exactly what he's done.

We don't view love this way, especially love from the Savior. Mary and Martha don't either. They tell him about their brother because they expect him to do something. They expect him to come running, like any friend or loved one would do for someone who is near their last breath. Can you imagine how you'd feel? *Up to this point, Jesus, I've witnessed you raise others from the dead. I know you turned water into wine and healed people possessed by demons. I know what you are capable of. Where in the world are you?*

In her book *Confronting Christianity*, Rebecca McLaughlin writes that one of the hang-ups people have with trusting Jesus is the suffering this world brings. You don't have to live long to see unimaginable suffering fall on the just and unjust.

> For many, this question torpedoes the Christian faith. How can the hypothesis of a loving, powerful God stand under the crushing weight of human distress? Does Christianity work only for those whose lives are not shipwrecked? Must we gloss over others' distress to believe in an omnipotent, benevolent Creator?
>
> . . . [the Christian worldview suggests] that suffering is not the wrecking ball that knocks Christianity down but rather the cornerstone on which, painfully, brick by brick, it has always been built.[1]

Innocent people suffer. Children die. Tragedy strikes when we're least expecting it. The world hears that God is love yet experiences the opposite. We don't live in Eden, and the world is a broken place. The suffering we experience, and the suffering those around us experience, screams that God can't be loving. If anything threatens our belief in Christ it's this—sometimes suffering never goes away. Sometimes we ask God for healing, and he delays. Sometimes we ask God for life, and we get death instead.

McLaughlin says that Jesus's interaction with Lazarus and his sisters in John 11 actually proves that Christianity is believable. She writes, "Suffering is not an embarrassment to the Christian faith. It is the thread with which Christ's name is stitched into our very lives."[2] As we will see, these sisters feel forgotten by Jesus. They feel as if he failed to show up for them. I suppose, you could say, it even feels embarrassing. Mary and Martha called out in faith and their brother died anyway. How do you show your face in Bethany when everyone knows this miracle man didn't come to work a miracle for you?

This is how we find Mary and Martha when we meet them in the second scene.

When Jesus Gives You Something Different

Jesus departs for Bethany knowing Lazarus is dead. At first read, this loss in John 11 feels heartless. But that's only if you don't know what's coming. Dale Ralph Davis says, "Jesus comes into our cemeteries with the best of news."[3] As he descends upon the funeral scene, you can feel the weight of death. By the time Jesus arrives, Lazarus has been buried in the tomb four days (v. 17). Jesus arrives to a mourning site. Friends have come to comfort the sisters. It's a community affair. In Jesus's day, funerals were multi-day events, with professional mourners, instruments, and loud cries. In our modern culture, we hide our grief behind church buildings and private burials, visitations, and funeral parlors. But for ancient Israel, death was an enemy to scream against. Perhaps the grief is compounded by the fact that this was all avoidable.

It's worth paying attention to the pace of this text. Jesus steps into Bethany, and Martha runs to him when she hears he's arrived.

Remember, she asked him to come. By this point, it's been at least four days since she sent a message to him, and it wasn't a four-day journey from Jerusalem. The text is clear to tell us the distance (two miles). She knows, and John wants the reader to know, the only reason Jesus took four days to get there is because he wanted to. This cuts like a knife to a woman who put all her eggs in the basket of her friend Jesus. When she asked him to come, it was because she knew he loved her brother. If he doesn't come heal him for friendship, what hope does she have that he can ever be motivated to come to them again?

While she's clearly brokenhearted, there doesn't seem to be bitterness toward Jesus for delaying. Imagine yourself in her shoes. Her brother is dead. She asked Jesus to help her, and he arrives four days too late. He's her friend, and even when friends hurt us, we want to run to them in our grief. She can't write him off as useless. But Jesus is no ordinary friend. When she meets him on the road, she comes with an honest question, crying, "If you had been here, my brother wouldn't have died" (v. 21). She still trusts that Jesus can do something for her family in the very next verse: "Yet even now I know that whatever you ask from God, God will give you" (v. 22). Do you hear her hope? Her brother lies cold in the tomb, but there is a shred of belief left. *Jesus loves her, this she knows.*

One would expect that the next move is resurrection. Lazarus died on his watch, but Jesus has come to make things right. Martha knows he can do it. The expectation is thick in this scene.

What feels like love is Jesus rushing into this "cemetery," calling Lazarus out immediately. But Jesus takes his time. In some scenes in John, he heals people quickly, like the case of the man who is lame in John 5. And in John 9, he heals a man born blind without him really asking. But here, when Mary and Martha plead with Jesus to do something, expecting that surely he'd be faster for them than he would be for those he barely knew, they are disappointed. They had asked him to come. And when he finally arrives, he's too late. Their brother is dead, and they're undone. *If you'd been here, Jesus.*

Is Jesus still someone to believe in when our cries seem to fall on deaf ears?

Robin prayed a similar prayer as Martha, separated by thousands of years of history. As a young wife and mom, she was troubled by her husband's frequent migraines and balance issues. After months of tests, they received a diagnosis—a rare disease with no cure. The only hope was maintenance, but the progression would be swift. The grief compounded when they found out the disease was genetic. Her sons likely inherited it.

The question loomed over her soul: *Jesus loves me, but if he'd been here, would this have happened?*

Even with the diagnosis and suffering, I know whatever you ask from God will be done; help me, Jesus, she thought to herself.

Like Mary and Martha, Robin had to hold her reality against the truth she knew about Jesus. He could have prevented this. He could have fixed this. Like this family in John, Robin's family is loved by Jesus. They are his people.

"I felt like God had forgotten me," she said. "I said to God, 'I paid my tithes, I took my family to church, and you've forgotten about me.'" All hope seemed lost when they received confirmation that her two sons had the same progressive, incurable disease. They faced the same fate as their father—a life of tumors, pain, repeat bouts of cancer, and multiple surgeries.

"I didn't want to live," she told me. "I had this thought, *We will all just get in the car and go together*. I didn't think I could face what we were facing." Her dad stood by her through the many nights in the hospital. As he slept on the floor of the ICU waiting room with her, he reminded her that he could pray with her, but she needed to also pray for peace that only God could grant. She didn't ask for this suffering. In fact, she asked for the exact opposite. She wanted a sweet life with her young sons and their father—all in good health. But she felt abandoned by God, in the sense of his absence it felt like a punishment. *If you'd been here, Jesus, we wouldn't be here.*

"Man was telling us one thing, but God ultimately had the plan for our future," she recalls. Doctors gave them a prognosis, but Robin grew to trust that only God could direct their outcome. In the moments of being shaken with the news of her new normal, she ran to God. She ran to the Savior, the one she begged to come and who delayed his relief. In those early days, she had two choices. She could have given in to the pain, turned the car on in the garage, and left it all behind. But instead, she chose the path toward the One to believe in, even when she couldn't see how he was believable in that moment.

Robin's husband and sons still live with this condition. There is no cure—in this life. How do we respond when our heart says, *If you had been here, we wouldn't be here*?

When all hope seems lost in our suffering, how do we find him believable? That's the question that was before Robin. It's the question before those tempted to unbelief as Rebecca McLaughlin writes. It's the question before us as we walk through this broken life. And it's the question before Mary and Martha.

Let's look at how Jesus answers it.

What the Savior Says

The beauty of looking at Jesus all throughout John is that we see his ability to adapt to people based on their needs in the moment. He doesn't change, but his responses change depending on the person. Jesus responds to these two sisters in two different ways.

Martha believes Jesus could have saved him, but her words carry a tinge of disappointment. *It didn't have to be this way, Jesus.*

We will see his interaction with Mary in a bit, but Tim Keller says that Jesus is adept at saying the right words for the right moment for each person. In other words, Keller, says, he gives Martha truth.[4]

"Your brother will rise again," Jesus says (John 11:23). Like every other interaction in John, she's confused. She's a follower of Jesus, so she knows what's to come. She doesn't doubt his ability or even his authority as the Messiah.

When Jesus gives her this truth about Lazarus's future, Martha responds with the only belief she has—background knowledge. "I know that he will rise again in the resurrection at the last day," she says in response (v. 24). Understanding Jesus's words is often a progressive experience for all of us, including Martha. Initially her belief is grounded in what she knows about the future, given her theology. She aligned with a school of Jewish belief that resurrection was coming to God's chosen people at the end of time. So, to hear that Lazarus will one day rise again is, for her, not likely a surprising thing to hear at a funeral. She knows it's true, so she's probably nodding along with Jesus at this point, believing in that grand future that God will bring one day for all believers, rather than believing in what Jesus is about to do for her right then. How does Jesus respond to her theological statement about the future and final resurrection that she knows is coming one day? He makes it clear that this "one day" she hopes so much in is wrapped up in one person. Himself. He gives her another "I AM" statement—"*I am* the resurrection and the life. The one who believes in me, even if he dies, will live" (v. 25, emphasis added). He gives her more truth—not just about the future of her brother, but about his own identity and power.

D. A. Carson writes,

> Jesus' concern is to divert Martha's focus from an abstract belief in what takes place on the last day, to a personalized belief in him who alone can provide it. Just as he not only gives the bread from heaven (6:27) but is himself the bread of life (6:35), so also he not only raises the dead on the last day (5:21, 25ff.) but is himself resurrection and the life. There is neither resurrection nor eternal life outside of him.[5]

In every interaction he has, Jesus is after meeting a person's desire so that they may find him someone to believe in. Köstenberger says, "The space between Lazarus's death and Jesus's calling of him out of the tomb is the space in which Martha sees Jesus for who he really is: her very life."[6]

Jesus expands on his "I AM" statement by telling Martha death is not the end, not for Lazarus and not for her. She believes in a future resurrection, and Jesus says, "Resurrection is here."

> "Do you believe this, Martha?"
>
> "I believe." (v. 27)

Two simple words carry profound meaning. Martha needed her idea about Jesus clarified so she could see him rightly. She believed in him as a friend and miracle worker, but she needed to *believe* in him the way John 20:31 says to believe in him—"I believe you are the Messiah, the Son of God, who comes into the world."

This is astounding given the circumstances. Martha believes while her brother lies cold in a grave. She believes before she sees the result of her belief. She believes before the miracle, not after. She's grieving, and confused at Jesus's delay, but that doesn't keep her from continuing to come to him. Loss, especially loss we asked God to prevent, leaves us feeling apprehensive around him. We thought we could trust him and now we wonder if we were wrong. He gave the opposite of what we prayed for, so we keep him at a safe distance.

Martha doesn't do that. She's hurt that he didn't show up, but she keeps running to him. She comes with honest questions and a broken heart. She follows in the footsteps of other believers, like the psalmists, who take their questions, confusion, loss, and grief to the foot of the Savior. Even without the answer yet, coming to him with our questions is a sign of belief. We wouldn't come to him if we didn't believe he could fix our predicament.

Martha doesn't have the outcome, but she trusts him. Martha doesn't have her prayer answered, but she finds his words to be believable—she finds *him* to be believable.

R. C. Sproul writes, "I don't think there is a greater confession of faith anywhere in Scripture than this confession that Martha made in the midst of sorrow. She had seen Jesus' miracles and heard His authoritative teaching, and she had believed He was who He said He was."[7]

There comes a point for many of us where we come to the fork in the road of belief. We don't know how it will end, but we have the truth. We don't know what's coming, but we must make a confession. Martha is a model for us, saying through tears and grief, "I believe." Robin had to stand before the unknown future of her husband and sons, saying through pain, "I believe."

The same is true for us. Resurrection was always God's plan for his people once sin entered the world. Now we have the living embodiment of resurrection in front of us in Jesus asking us to trust him when we can't see what's next.

What the Savior Feels

Jesus gives Martha truth, as Keller says. But he gives Mary something different.

Martha calls for her sister to come see Jesus. You see the differences between these sisters in this text, but you also see their differences elsewhere (Luke 10:38–42). Martha is what we would call the "bossy" one, and Mary is the "quiet" one. Martha wears her heart on her sleeve, but she also gets things done. Mary feels deeply, but she also needs moments of retreat. Jesus knows how to minister to both.

Jesus pivots from truth-telling when Mary rushes to him. It's interesting that Mary comes saying the same thing as her sister, "Lord, if you had been here, my brother wouldn't have died!" (John 11:32). But Jesus doesn't respond to her like he does Martha.

John moves from telling us what Jesus says to giving us a window into his soul. In a span of five verses, we learn that Jesus is "deeply moved and troubled" twice and that he weeps. He gives Mary no words; he just feels with her. He sits with her in her grief.

The contrast between the two sisters shows the dexterity of our Savior. He can give people what they need, sometimes within seconds of each other. He knows his own intimately, so he speaks and ministers to them—showing them his love and care for them.

But we lose some of the power of Jesus's response to Mary in our English translation of the words *deeply moved*. The Christian Standard Bible includes a footnote to include that this word could also mean "angry." In fact, D. A. Carson says Jesus is outraged. Other theologians speak to the rage Jesus has in this moment.[8]

The question then becomes "Why is he so mad?" Have you ever been to a funeral and felt rage? A few years ago, a friend of mine tragically died in an accident. He had stopped on the side of the road to help a stranded motorist and was struck by an eighteen-wheeler. The tragedy was compounded by the fact that he was traveling to pick up an old car to work on with his son. The days following his death were a blur. It made no sense to me. This was a man cut down in the prime of his life. He pastored a growing church plant, had four amazing kids, loved his wife. He was a good friend to all who knew him. I'll never forget the last conversation I had with him in person. He encouraged me to keep pressing on in ministry. And then he looked me in the eye and said, "I'm really proud of you." The news is littered with stories of unfaithful pastors and leaders who disappoint us. My friend was one of the good ones—and then he was just gone.

When I finally let myself feel the grief and shock of his passing, I wept in our bed one night, saying repeatedly "I don't understand. I don't understand." Because of the pandemic, I couldn't travel for his funeral, but watched it online. Seeing his wife—also my friend—and children worship and weep brought the same emotions up in me. But it also made me so angry. *If you had been there, Jesus, John wouldn't have died.*

But he was there. And he is there.

I think Jesus felt all of it with me. I know he felt all of it with my friend's wife and small children. In John 1, we're told that Jesus was there at the beginning. He's the one who created all things and upholds all things with his word. Isn't he angry when the world he created groans for redemption? When the people he spoke into existence are cut down too soon, leaving grieving families in their absence. Isn't he angry when the effects of this sin-cursed world ravage us on all sides? As the great Christmas carol says, "He comes to make his blessings flow far as the curse is found," so when he sees the curse run amok, he's angry—and he weeps.[9]

That he would weep with us is remarkable. But here's the even more remarkable part: in Martha's case, he weeps knowing what he is about to do. Within minutes, he's going to fix the problem of death for this family. But that doesn't mean he doesn't feel the pain of it before he reverses it. The lesson for us here is an important one as we struggle with loss in this life. Like Mary and Martha, we know that those we love will rise again if they're trusting in Christ. They might not rise quickly, but it's as certain as the rising sun that they will. This doesn't remove the ache their death brings. We can grieve in hope, but we still grieve. We can know life is waiting for us because of Christ, but we still rage against death itself. It's the most unnatural thing we experience. We were meant to live, so every encounter with death is a flashing sign that things are not right—and we're desperate for Christ to make all things new. If Jesus is angry over something he knows he's fixing soon, how much more should we be angry over the same thing?

We know he will end all suffering, but like these sisters, we live in the time between death and new life. And the pain of that time is acute. And Jesus gets that pain. He feels it with us.

With Martha we see the truth of Jesus, but with Mary we see his compassion. They aren't in competition, they simply come out when the situation warrants and together fill out a portrait of who our Savior truly is. The truth he told Martha didn't change when he encountered Mary. He knew what Mary needed most was his rage over her brother's sudden departure.

This is not how it's supposed to be, we can hear through his tears. And he's on a mission to fix it.

What the Savior Does

Throughout the Gospel of John, Jesus makes statements about his "hour" or his "time." When people want Jesus to act, he often says, "My hour has not yet come." Shortly after this scene, Jesus changes course and acknowledges that his hour is indeed now upon them. This refers to his appointment with death and the cross, but the principle is an important one. Jesus is controlled by no one. When he and the Father decide it's time, it's time. When he moves to save, he saves. When he comes to heal and restore, it happens. Not a moment sooner and not a minute too late.

Another theme in John is glory. Often, Jesus is not ready to "glorify" himself, meaning he's not ready for everyone to see the full picture of his identity. His "hour" hasn't come. Except here, he says "I told you if you believed you would see the glory of God."

And after giving his friends what they needed—truth and tears—he finally gives them what they have begged him for—the life of their brother.

Here's how the climax of the story unfolds:

> Then Jesus, deeply moved again, came to the tomb. It was a cave, and a stone lay against it. Jesus said, "Take away the stone." Martha, the sister of the dead man, said to him, "Lord, by this time there will be an odor, for he has been dead four days." Jesus said to her, "Did I not tell you that if you believed you would see the glory of God?" So they took away the stone. And Jesus lifted up his eyes and said, "Father, I thank you that you have heard me. I knew that you always hear me, but I said this on account of the people standing around, that they may believe that you sent me." When he had said these things, he cried out with a loud voice, "Lazarus, come out." (John 11:38–43 ESV)

You can imagine the dead silence after that resounding command rings out of Jesus's mouth. The collective breath of the funeral attendants held in, afraid to exhale. The eyes of all darting back and forth between Jesus and the tomb. *What's going to happen?*

> The man who had died came out, his hands and feet bound with linen strips, and his face wrapped with a cloth. Jesus said to them, "Unbind him, and let him go." (v. 44 ESV)

Just as he did with all his other "I AM" statements, Jesus makes it clear who he is. *If you are thirsty, I can satisfy you, he says. If you're hungry, I'm the bread of life. If you're lost and scared and hurt, I'm the Good Shepherd. And if it's life you're looking for—I am life itself, able to grant it to whoever I want. Cisterns will run dry and bread will mold and leaders will fail, but I am someone to believe in.*

My kids love this story. It's a great story to tell children because they can use their "outside" voices to reenact the scene, screaming for Lazarus to come out. But the wonder of it is not only that Lazarus came back to life. It's that Jesus waited so long. Lazarus has been in the tomb four days before Jesus resurrects him. He didn't come immediately. He waited until Lazarus's death was a certainty. He let the family know their brother was dead and gone before he moved to action. It took forty-four verses, and countless tears and questions, for the prayers of these sisters to be answered.

They wept for days waiting for Jesus to come. They came to him with pleading statements of sadness and confusion. He didn't fix it immediately. We can read the Lazarus story and marvel that a dead man walked out of the tomb, but let's also marvel at a Savior who delays and lets his beloved children sit in grief while they learn more of his character.

That's a hard place to live if you're in it. And as Rebecca McLaughlin said, many are unwilling to entertain belief because they see so many people living in the in-between space, waiting for Jesus to show up at their funeral scene.

Jesus Gives Them What They Need, Not How They Want It

These women thought what they needed from Jesus was healing. But what they really needed from him was resurrection. And you only get that by dying first. The story moves fast when you read it, but at an agonizing pace when you live it.

Their brother literally died, and that was devastating. But their expectation of the Messiah was buried in that tomb too. He was preparing them for what was next. This wouldn't be the first tomb that held the body of a man they loved. Jesus was on his way to the tomb too. And Lazarus was a picture of what Jesus would do in a matter of months with his own body.

They had to walk through suffering to get life. They had to see the grave to see the empty tomb. The same is true for us. How many of us have stories of suffering that birthed hope in us? Even my friend John who died in the tragic accident. He's in glory now, experiencing a relationship with the Savior I can only anticipate and long for. But he didn't get there apart from deep loss. His family still lives with that ache. Mary and Martha's story wraps up nicely at the end of John 11, but some of us are still standing in the funeral scene. The Savior is there weeping with us too.

Tish Harrison Warren writes, "We live in view of death so that we might live in light of the hope of new life—knowing that the only way to resurrection is through darkness."[10] She goes on to write, "We are dying, each and all. Yet the kind of blessing we most need is the kind that comes to the dying—a blessing we live our life avoiding, a blessing found only in darkness. In the place of deepest desolation, we meet God himself."[11]

Isn't that what Mary and Martha experienced? There is no greater darkness than the death of someone you love. Nothing is more permanent than when you lower the casket in the ground and cover it with dirt. There is no coming back from the grave. In burial, you say goodbye to relationship, dreams, the life you had, and the simple things like the sound of their laugh. Mary and Martha expected resurrection, but they expected it long after they also were buried in the tomb with their brother. They weren't looking for life that day. They were looking for comfort.

Jesus gave them that, and so much more.

I'm sure you have stories of Jesus delaying in your own life. Where what feels loving to you is the exact opposite of what Jesus does. Maybe even right now, Jesus is delaying. He is giving you the hard thing, instead of answering your request.

And you're left with feeling like he doesn't love you—like the light is not shining in the darkness.

One of my favorite books to read with my kids is *Dangerous Journey*, the children's version of *Pilgrim's Progress*. In the final chapter, Christian walks through one last trial before he reaches heaven's shores. He must walk through the waters to the other side, but as he begins the journey, the waters only rise. As he moves across the "River of Death," he's understandably scared. He can't feel the bottom. He doesn't know where the waters end and the shore begins. He begins to scream and flail about, thinking this must be the end. Every battle fought on this journey, every temptation overcome, and every truth claimed in the quest for glory is for naught. He can't see how he will endure to the end. And as he is about to give up hope, the ground stabilizes beneath him. He feels land. And in that moment, he says,

> But the troubles a man goes through in these waters are no sign that God has forsaken him.[12]

After all the faithfulness on his journey, in that crisis he wondered if God had forgotten him when he needed him most. I wonder if that's how Mary and Martha felt when they asked Jesus to come, and he delayed. In John 11 and for all who trust in Christ, death is no sign that God has forgotten you. His love is not determined by his immediate action—because God plays the long game with us. For Mary and Martha, they did not have to wait long for Jesus to bring resurrection hope. But for all of us, we're still waiting for the resurrection. If we haven't already, we will all bury people we love; and when their bodies are lowered in the ground, it will feel like God has forgotten us. His delay does not mean the promise isn't coming. Like the father in Mark, we can say through tears, "I do believe; help my unbelief!" (Mark 9:24). The Lord has a future hope for us—a resurrection for us—and he will show up in the last day to resurrect all who hope in him.

Martha gets the truth. Mary gets the tears. And Lazarus gets to live.

We will too.

11

He Will Make a Home for You

John 14

HAVE YOU EVER BEEN to a funeral for an unbeliever? It's a tragic scene. Every eulogy, testimony, and story about the person is an attempt to alleviate any concern about their final destination. *There has to be a way to show they made it to heaven, or to the other side.* I once attended a funeral for a man who spent most of his life in church, but bore little fruit, if any. None of his children had anything to share about him. The pastor who did the funeral, only knew him from the occasional visit to church with his wife. When one family member spoke about his eternal resting place, he appealed to this man's good works. He was nice. He loved people. He loved to laugh. He knew how to work hard.

None of that, Jesus says, gets you to where he's going.

Throughout this book, we've looked at Jesus as someone to believe in from a variety of angles. Jesus is the same yesterday, today, and forever. Who he is in our past is the same as right now. It's easy to recount how he's provided for us yesterday (or last year). And in our clearest moments we see his provision in the moment. But trusting him for what we haven't yet seen is hard. We're like people standing at the base of a mountain, straining our eyes to see the trees at the top. We know they're there, but we've never hiked that mountain. We're going on the word of a friend, or a guidebook, to assure us that life exists at the peak.

We need to know life exists on the other side of the mountain. Jesus gave many promises to his disciples before he left them. The reverberating promise in these last moments with them is that he wouldn't leave them to fend for themselves. To put it in a phrase, there is no gap in his presence among them. They may feel his absence physically, but they get something better with his presence inside them. He is taking up residence in them, so they will never be alone.

This was important because life was about to get hard. By the time John writes his Gospel, all the disciples are gone. Some died of old age, but most died a martyr's death. John is the last man standing. John recounts Jesus's words, "I will not leave you as orphans, I am coming to you," (John 14:18), and this is not just theory to him. He's lived it.

What Jesus Means

In John 14, the disciples are visibly shaken. Jesus tells them he's leaving them and they can't go with him. We unpacked his promises to them in chapter 6, but if you look at John 14 closely, you may notice that I left out a couple of key verses in the chapter on John 13–16.

Jesus provides another comfort to his disciples as he readies them for his absence. In John 14:1–3, Jesus says:

> "Don't let your hearts be troubled. Believe in God; believe also in me. In my Father's house are many rooms. If it were not so, would I have told you that I am going to prepare a place for you? If I go away

> and prepare a place for you, I will come again and take you to myself, so that where I am you may be also."

Right before this, Jesus has an interaction with Peter. You may remember it from chapter 6, where he tells Peter that within hours he will deny Jesus three times (John 13:36–38). Then before that, they discover that one of their friends will betray Jesus that night. Then before that, Jesus says, "This is our last meal together for a while."

It makes sense that anxiety is the prevailing feeling. They're still processing this news, and their faces must show their distress. In addition to promising them his continual presence, he also promises them that he has work to do on their behalf. Jesus isn't leaving them so he can go back to the comfort of heaven. He's going to get heaven ready for them.

I grew up listening to a collection of Scriptures set to song by Steve Green. One song rings in my ears every time I read this passage. "In my Father's house are many mansions, many mansions in my Father's house." This is taken from the King James Version, but it has led to many believing that there is a nice home waiting for them when they get to heaven. Maybe you've also wondered if heaven would be an upgrade from your current living situation. Although we don't have every detail of heaven, I don't think Jesus's point is that our dream home awaits us when we die. The kingdom of heaven is not open concept living/kitchen combo and a master bedroom on the main floor. Jesus is showing the kind of Savior he is when he assures the disciples there is a home outside the home they can see here.

Various translations use different words for "place" and "rooms." Some say that Jesus is preparing a "dwelling place." But the point here is the preparation Jesus undergoes to get them to this final resting place. D. A. Carson writes, "It is not that he arrives on the scene and then begins to prepare the place; rather, in the context of Johannine theology, it is the going itself, via the cross and resurrection, that prepares the place for Jesus' disciples. And if he takes such trouble, all to prepare a place for his own, it is inconceivable that the rest should not follow: *I will come back and take you to be with me that you may also be where I am.*"[1]

In other words, if he's willing to give his life to prepare a place for them, how much more can they trust him to finish what he started? As Paul says in Romans 8:32, if he didn't spare his own Son to save you, how much more can you trust him to provide everything else? The point is not the rooms themselves. The point is the Savior who gets the rooms ready. And if he's getting your place ready, he will be faithful to bring you safely to the other side (Rom. 8:38).

The Message paraphrases John 14:1–3 this way:

> "Don't let this rattle you. You trust God, don't you? Trust me. There is plenty of room for you in my Father's home. If that weren't so, would I have told you that I'm on my way to get a room ready for you? And if I'm on my way to get your room ready, I'll come back and get you so you can live where I live. And you already know the road I'm taking."

As we know by now, John's entire aim throughout the whole book is belief. This discourse is one more proof that Jesus is worthy of our trust. His departure and absence are only temporary. One day, the union we experience with Christ through the Spirit will be a union we experience in the flesh. We will live with him, in a place he prepared for us.

But the disciples have a lot of questions. Thomas says what everyone is thinking: "Lord, we don't know where you're going. How can we know the way?" (John 14:5). It's reasonable to make this statement. Everything Jesus tells them is new and outside their understanding of the kingdom. Like Nicodemus, they thought their Jewishness was enough. Like Martha, they thought resurrection was coming in the last day. Like the Jewish people, they thought the kingdom was coming right then.

Jesus introduces another powerful "I AM" statement to make it real to them. "I am the way, the truth, and the life. No one comes to the Father except through me" (John 14:6). In other words, we have no need to fear that there won't be enough rooms for us because Jesus is clearing our path to the neighborhood.

Where I live it's not uncommon to see a homeless person at a stoplight. It doesn't matter your neighborhood; homelessness is no respecter of zip codes. The Covid-19 pandemic, high interest rates, and low inventory have only exacerbated an existing crisis. When we drive past these men, women, and (sometimes) children, my own children often ask what their signs say, or why they're asking for money on the side of the road.

My kids have never known homelessness. They've lived in two houses since their birth. Whenever we bring up the possibility of moving again at some point, they revolt. They love our home. They're comfortable here. They feel safe.

Homelessness is a particularly traumatic experience. In the absence of a stable environment to return to each day, homeless people face additional setbacks and complications beyond not having a roof over their heads. They face food insecurity because they have nowhere to store food, even if they had the money to buy it. This leads to unhealthy food options, which cause medical problems. On top of this, extreme weather conditions contribute to poor health. There are mental hurdles as well, like the stress of never knowing where you will sleep, protecting yourself from people who try to harm you, and the shame attached to homelessness. Homeless women and teens are far more likely to use their bodies for food or money, leaving them trapped in a lifestyle they can't escape.[2]

All that to say, the angst and questions the disciples feel and ask over the home Jesus makes for them is normal. Humans were made for the safety home provides, but also the stability. A loving home centers us. Home is where families are built, and people are welcomed. I don't wear my pajamas and no make-up just anywhere. But when my kids go to bed, the first thing I do is throw on comfy pajamas and wash my face.

When I travel, I never sleep as well in a hotel bed. And my first night back home is usually my best night of sleep. The absence of home leaves a void nothing else can fill.

This is why it's so comforting to read Jesus's words. He's not only making a home for us, but he's also providing the way into the house. He's the gate to heaven (John 10:9). The home he is preparing is only for those who know how to open the gate—who trust in him and are united to him by faith. The preparation he undergoes to get us to heaven is to first make us ready for heaven. And while we are separated from him in this life, he gives us assurance that it's only a temporary absence. We will be home one day.

Hope While We Wait

When I was a child, I loved visiting Great-Aunt Geri's house. Burying her only child in infancy, she welcomed any opportunity to have children in her home. Every Christmas, she gifted me another Barbie doll, fit with a dress handmade by her. But her home contained an entire room of Barbie dolls with an assortment of dresses that would keep me occupied for hours.

One weekend, my parents arranged for me to stay overnight with her. Like any eager child, I packed by bags and jumped at the chance for a weekend with more Barbies than I had time to play with. But like any innocent child, I didn't know what it would feel like to stay away from my home and my parents.

I didn't last the night.

There was nothing wrong at Aunt Geri's house. It just wasn't my house. What I could enjoy for a few hours on a Saturday felt impossible to endure overnight. My heart ached for my home. And I'm not alone. We—each one of us on this planet—experience a similar homesickness in this life. Indeed, deep within all of humankind is a collective homesickness for something better than what we experience here. Jen Pollock Michel is right when she says that our most human longing is to long for home.[3]

Scripture gives us a reason for this universal experience. Throughout the Bible, God's people are portrayed as exiles, aliens, even strangers in this world. The garden of Eden was our first home, that home was ruined by sin. Since then, God has been on a rescue mission to bring his people back home to him. In Hebrews 11, considered the great "hall of faith" chapter, we read how the biblical characters from Abraham onward died in faith. But they were never home here.

> These all died in faith, although they had not received the things that were promised. But they saw them from a distance, greeted them, and confessed that they were foreigners and temporary residents on the earth. Now those who say such things make it clear that they are seeking a homeland. If they were thinking about where they came from, they would have had an opportunity to return. But they now desire a better place—a

> heavenly one. Therefore, God is not ashamed to be called their God, for he has prepared a city for them. (Heb. 11:13–16)

And then again in Hebrews 13:14, the writer of Hebrews says: "For we do not have an enduring city here; instead, we seek the one to come." Jesus prepared the disciples before his departure for this reality. From that point forward, they would feel homesick. They could carry with them a deep ache for life with Jesus again. But he also gives them the assurance that their homesickness has a purpose. It's fitting them for glory.

We weren't made to be comfortable here. But that's not the way we operate sometimes, is it? Jesus doesn't tell the disciples that he goes to prepare a place for them in the fallen world as they know it. He tells them he goes to prepare a place for them with his Father. If this fallen world, and all that you love and experience here, leaves you wanting more, that's the point. Its fall from grace will always point you toward the home you were made for.

But it's not just a home in heaven that he's preparing for us. Jesus tells the disciples he goes to make a home for them, but he also promises to remake the home we have here one day. The promise of the home he makes for us includes his return to set right what was lost in Eden. God intended to dwell among his people, in a home he made for them. When we die, we go home to him. And one day, he will restore what was lost and bring his children to their perfect home in a new heaven and new earth (Revelation 21).

I taught high school for a couple of years before I had my twins, and I always told my students that their best days here pale in comparison to the days they will have in heaven. When they enjoy a good burger, or laugh at a funny joke, or find community with their friends, these are all foretastes of the home to come. When those things are removed, they feel an ache. But it's because they were never meant to be satisfied with earthly things. They are touchpoints of God's goodness toward them, but they are markers of home—a home we haven't inherited yet.

When Home Is Hard

The disciples understood the metaphor for home. In their culture, home was filled with family members, but not many rooms. I have four sons, and our home does not have enough bedrooms for all of them, so they share rooms. In Jesus's day, everyone shared rooms—even the parents and children. When he talks about the home he makes for them, there is room for everyone.

But there may be some reading this who feel differently about home. Maybe your home was not a safe place growing up, and your homesickness was for safety and security. Maybe your current home is full of resentment and fighting. Maybe you long for a place to call your own, but you live with roommates or don't have enough rooms for all your family members.

Or maybe your spiritual home, the church, has left you homesick. How can you long for a spiritual home with Jesus when you can't even find one on earth? If this life is supposed to be a foretaste of what is to come, spiritual and physical homesickness are an acute pain. How can you long for the home Jesus provides if you can't imagine a home here?

Physical homelessness is disorienting and hard to overcome. But spiritual homelessness causes wounds that no one may see, and hidden wounds are the hardest to heal.

We all have our own stories of finding faith communities wanting. The church is supposed to be our "home away from home." A living example of God's faithful witness to a watching world. It's where broken people find hope. It's where men and women who have nothing in common, join together to worship their older brother, Jesus Christ. We may be "aliens and strangers" on earth, but among God's people we're family (1 Pet. 2:11 NASB1995). This is why it hurts so badly when the family of God is dysfunctional. We're filled with cliques and factions that treat people like there really is no room for them in God's house. Mike Cosper writes, "This is one of the most complicated elements of our faith; the very people who can help us meet and know Jesus are also the ones who can hurt us at the deepest levels."[4]

When Jesus left his disciples on earth, he told them he would build his church through their witness and teaching (Matt. 28:18–20; John 21:17). The entire book of Acts is devoted to this mission, where the once scared and confused disciples become the bold and Spirit-filled apostles. The church in Acts, and throughout the Epistles, is filled with people who have nothing in common except everything. They eat together. They share resources and their lives. They hurt one another and then turn around and forgive one another.

They're a family living far from their true home. They're exiles, foreigners, aliens, and strangers in a land that was once familiar, but now should feel utterly foreign. We are no different today. At least we shouldn't be.

I think the reason we get off track is because we're so comfortable here. Home in this life makes a home we can't see less inviting, especially in the affluent West. But if these last few years have taught us anything, it's that the home we're making here is built on shaky foundation. It can crumble with the wind of political power and denominational authority. We think our homesickness is owing to losing influence. But really, our homesickness is because the home we've made here is a monster that always needs to be fed but is never satiated.

Maybe there is an ache inside you for home. Psalm 137:4 says, "How can we sing the LORD's song on foreign soil?" Or another way to say it is—how can we sing his song in a foreign land?

Russell Moore writes:

> If exile language is used to bemoan a "darkening" or "growingly hostile" culture, rather than to see our situation as fundamentally the same as every other era before us, then we don't understand what the Bible means by exile. . . . We are born into the kingdom of God, and so we are experiencing both some of the realities of the kingdom now *and* the longing for those which are yet to come. That reality makes up the paradox of what it means to be born again in the first place. We are in the world, and yet not of it. We are sinners, yet justified. We are dying, yet resurrected.[5]

The promise to the disciples was something they could anchor their faith on when home felt shaky. When Paul was in chains in prison, he knew Jesus had a room for him in heaven, a heavenly city "not made with hands" (2 Cor. 5:1). When Peter was crucified upside down, he knew it was just a few short hours to home. When division threatened the early church, the reminder of home sustained them. Peter reminds us repeatedly in 1 Peter, that we are citizens of heaven, we are a holy nation, we are a house for the Savior, and after we've "suffered a little while," he will one day take us home to a house that can never be taken from us (1 Pet. 5:10).

Sometimes we feel more exiled from our church community than we do the world. That's not what Jesus wants for his family. The home he's preparing for us has room enough for all, but it's not a mansion with one tribe on the east wing and the other tribe on the west. It's a home where we feast and gather around the marriage supper of the Lamb (Rev. 19:6–9). We feel a homesickness now because we're not there yet, and there is still pruning left to do in us and in our fellow brothers and sisters. In other words, the building project isn't finished.

A Picture of Home

I want to leave you with a story of hope. The church gets a bad rap today, and there are good reasons. It seems we can't go a week without another church scandal hitting the news. Pastors disappoint and abuse their power. Church members gossip and devour one another. Churches dissolve over disunity.

On top of it, churches are often not a picture of the family God is making. Martin Luther King Jr. is famous for saying that Sunday morning is the most segregated hour in America.[6] Jesus came to create a people from every tribe, tongue, and nation, but rarely do those tribes, tongues, and nations worship together.

This is why I love hearing my friend Edith's story. Edith was born in Mexico and came to America when she was six. Fleeing domestic violence, her mother crossed the border with her children in the hopes of a brighter future than what they had in Mexico.

They were on their way from Texas to the orchards in Michigan for work when their car broke down on Interstate 30 in Arkadelphia, Arkansas. If you've never heard of Arkadelphia, you're not the only one. The town has a McDonalds now, but even that was an upgrade when it was built. It's a small town that's only made larger by the two colleges that grow the population. Arkadelphia is not a place people flock to for refuge or even a new life.

What they found in Arkadelphia was a community and Christian faith they hold dear to this day. Though they never intended to stay in Arkadelphia long-term, the people at First Baptist Arkadelphia welcomed them, helped them find housing, and enroll Edith and her siblings in school. Eventually Edith's mom found a job and they began making their life there. But there was one significant barrier to settling permanently in America—they were not citizens. Stamped across their social security cards were the words *Not Valid for Employment*. They could attend school, but beyond that, they couldn't work or apply for financial aid when they attended college. Edith's mom could not move beyond her job at the poultry plant, and the family continued to live paycheck to paycheck.

Along the way, Edith became friends with a girl whose dad was a professor at the local Baptist university. This family welcomed Edith as their own, inviting her on family trips and even opening pathways for her to attend college and receive scholarships. Edith recalls,

> When I was with them, I didn't have to be responsible for ensuring the house was clean, my siblings were fed, my sister's hair was combed and that everyone got on the bus for school. For a lot of those early years, my mom worked the graveyard shift or the shift that began at 5:30 a.m. Either way, my mom would braid my hair before she left and then the rest was on me. It was hard, but it was our normal. When you're the oldest girl in the family and Mom is always working, you step up.

But with her friend's family, she could be a kid. The parents were observant, so they did everything they could to alleviate some of that burden for Edith. They also knew that Edith and her family were in America illegally, which filled each day with anxiety. One wrong move or statement, and they could be exposed and deported.

The road to citizenship or permanent residency is difficult, and often the only way is if an employer is willing to petition for your visa, or going back to your home country while you apply for residency. Going home was not an option for Edith's family. She had three siblings who were American citizens, as well as fears over the violence they had to flee when she was a child.

Over the years, her friend's family wrote letters to petition a change in their status to no avail.

Then one day the worst happened.

In a raid on her mom's employment, immigration picked up Edith's mom and everyone else in the plant who was illegal. Up to this point, they had been able to fly under the radar, but now their immigration status was exposed. And Edith's mom was locked up facing deportment. Her first phone calls were to her friend's mom and her pastor. They stood by Edith and her siblings as they worked to get her mom released. Then the miraculous happened, her mom was one of seven people released (with no charges or threat of deportment). Then a year later, the judge canceled her threat of deportment and instead granted her permanent residency.

At first it seemed their years of anxiety over being deported were over, but immigration doesn't work that way. Even though Edith's mom received residency status, it had no bearing on Edith's or her siblings' status. They were not truly safe.

Throughout her time in Arkadelphia, the constant anchor for her was her Christian community. The church was her first access point to American life. Her friend in class was her model for friendship and community. The Baptist college welcomed her with support and care. She came to America without a permanent home but found one among brothers and sisters in Christ. God gave her a home and a place to belong.

This became even more important as she began her fight for permanent residency in 2009, four years after her mom received her own status change. While she was able to attend school with her social security card, it still said *Not Valid for Employment* across the top. When her friends talked about internships and job opportunities after graduation, Edith silently wondered if she would ever be able to move beyond a paycheck-to-paycheck life. But her Christian community did not give up on helping her find a complete home here in America. They believed so strongly that she was one of them, that they worked tirelessly to make her place in Arkadelphia permanent. She told me of their efforts to help her gain citizenship:

> In 2009, everything came together. I had met Abby, an OBU student, when she tutored me in junior high. She was living in DC and had a connection with an immigration officer. He agreed to let us surrender to him and he would release us that same day after processing us. The Lord's timing was impeccable. The officer was going to be promoted within days of us surrendering. The morning of June 24th, Mrs. Kluck and Mrs. Baldwin drove us to a remote location. It was the same detention center my mom was taken to four years earlier. The detention center was cold with cells not much bigger than a standard office with a toilet on the one side with no privacy doors. Had Mrs. Kluck and Mrs. Baldwin not been outside, I might have been even more frightened than I was. Yet somehow I simultaneously had peace. I had prayed and cried and prayed some more for a way to naturalization. But this was barely the beginning. The hard work came fast building a case to gain permanent residency. We had to demonstrate that being deported would be a hardship to my mother, now a permanent resident and my three younger US-born siblings. We also had to prove

> good moral character, and our community came together to speak up for us. It seemed as if everyone was willing to write letters of recommendation for us. It was really heartwarming to read these. A few OBU professors wrote letters on my behalf.

When their car broke down in Arkadelphia all those years ago, they never imagined that would be their permanent home. They thought they were just passing through on the way to a better life. But they found a home there because God's people were there. God showed his heart of welcome to them through his church. He made a home for them.

The Liminal Space

I hear of homelessness among Christians all the time. Maybe it's the rise of social media and rapid news dissemination that leads us to think we're in a greater crisis and longing for our true home than any other time in recent memory. Or maybe God's people have always been living with this ache for something better. At least the Bible paints it that way. Where I live, in the Bible Belt, there is a comfortability that comes with being a Christian. We don't have to suffer that much for following Christ.

As I've tried to unpack in this chapter, we might not face threat of violence for claiming the name of Christ, but we certainly face strife for breaking rank with our "tribes." Rarely a week goes by that I don't hear from friends who are left reeling from losing their Christian community. Sometimes it's over church conflict. Other times it's over lack of transparency among leadership. We differ on politics and application of Scripture. Priorities and philosophies of ministry change. And sometimes, it's more nefarious, like abuse cover-up or outright lying.

There are a lot of homeless Christians.

Recently, I talked with a friend about how disoriented I felt looking for a new church home. Everything felt foreign to us. I had no job. We had no Christian community to call our own. And every Sunday we stepped foot into a church building that we did not know to worship alongside people who didn't know us.

We felt homeless.

She then gave me an image that she'd had another friend give her in a similar season. She said it was like we were in a canoe in the middle of the ocean. Behind us was the land we left behind, and we knew there was land ahead, but we couldn't quite make it out yet. We were just drifting in our canoe toward the shore of this unknown land—this unknown home. It was our liminal space, the time between the home we knew and the home we needed. Maybe that's how you feel on this journey toward home. The home you once knew doesn't feel like home anymore. The home you're hoping for isn't in sight yet, but you know it's coming. You can't drift forever.

Jesus's words to us in John 14 anchor us as we drift along toward home. But packaged within John 14 is another promise that we already looked at in this book—he's with us. We won't remain homeless forever, but he's given us a temporary shelter as we wait for our permanent space. The Spirit is with us in the liminal space. He takes shelter in us so he can be our shelter in our homelessness.

All the risks of homelessness in our society aren't risks for us in our spiritual lives. Physical homelessness is devastating, but for the believer, spiritual homelessness is impossible. We always have our brother with us, making his home in us, on this pilgrim journey home. The exile has an end-date. A better home is coming. As we've seen all along the way in this journey through John, Jesus finishes everything he starts. On the cusp of overwhelming grief and pain, the Savior looks outward to his fearful friends, who feel this liminal space acutely. D. A. Carson writes:

> It is Jesus who is heading for the agony of the cross; it is Jesus who is deeply "troubled" in heart (12:27) and spirit (13:21). Yet on this night of nights, when of all times it would have been appropriate for Jesus' followers to lend him emotional and spiritual support, he is still the one who gives, comforts, instructs. For they, too, are *troubled* (same verb as the verses just cited)—not because they are rushing toward pain, ignominy, shame, crucifixion, but because they are confused, uncertain of what Jesus means, and threatened by references to his imminent departure. However appropriate it may be to cite the words *Do not let your hearts be troubled* at Christian funerals, they were first addressed to disciples who under substantial emotional pressure were on the brink of catastrophic failure.[7]

He could have thought only about himself that night. The pain he was to face superseded the emotional pain they anticipated. But he didn't. He set his face and heart toward them. Just like he laid aside his glory to stoop low and come to earth, he laid aside his pain to alleviate theirs.

We are homeless, but it's a temporary exile. Jesus is getting our home ready. Until then, he's with us in the liminal space while we drift toward home.

12

The Bread of Life Gives Me Hope

God's people are frequently called to remember his goodness to them. When everyone else looks forward, we practice remembrance. But there is a unique struggle in remembering God in the every day. I enjoy running but hold a particular hatred for running hills. And that's a bummer because I live in a neighborhood surrounded by hills. Standing at the bottom of a hill, knowing I must run up it, I lose all sense of belief that the run is worth it. I'd rather quit. What helps me in the present is a belief about the future. Making it up the hill is painful, hard, and not my favorite. But I know a downward run awaits on the other side. I know there is beauty at the top of the hill. I know that my training up to this point prepared me to run the hill.

The same is true for belief. We're wrapping up a section looking at Jesus's believability for our present, and as we saw in the previous section, God continues to show his people that he can be trusted. I want to introduce you to two women, Heidi and Tracy. Both women have walked through lifelong suffering but keep jogging along up the hill—believing that there is hope in the present because of what awaits them on the other side.

Heidi's Story

Heidi was twenty-three years old when her entire world turned upside down. She was newly married and like any young married woman, dreamed about the life that was ahead of her. Instead, she was diagnosed with a benign brain tumor that led to decades of brain-related traumas and struggles. When I talked to Heidi, she shared about God's faithfulness to her through every surgery, doctor visit, and post-operative rehabilitation. But it was a deep loss one year after her initial tumor-removal surgery that her belief was challenged to the core.

> When I reached the year anniversary of my original tumor-removal surgery, my neurosurgeon cleared me to start trying to get pregnant. My husband and I were thrilled to find out just a month later that I was expecting our first child. After all we had endured throughout that past year, we were particularly relieved and overjoyed to be walking toward growing our family. At the 8-week mark of my pregnancy, I had some bleeding, but an ultrasound showed a strong heartbeat and growing baby. About two weeks later when I went in for a regular appointment and another ultrasound, after what felt like some endless moments of silence from my doctor, he told me he could not find a heartbeat. He called another doctor in to confirm that our baby had indeed died in my womb. The child we had wanted so badly and the joy that had come after a year filled with trauma was suddenly gone.
>
> Both my husband and I grieved the loss of that child, but in different ways. For me, one of the lies

> I started to believe was that God had taken our child because I had failed to learn something that he wanted me to learn throughout my brain journey. I was doubting God's goodness just months after seeing his faithfulness in truly miraculous ways and experiencing his nearness more than I could have ever imagined.
>
> The same day I found out I had lost my baby I was set to give my testimony at Bible study. It was the first time I planned to talk about my brain tumor publicly. I had chosen 1 Peter 5 ("after you have suffered a little while"). There were trials and hardships I thought I was talking about that night, but I gave that testimony with that dead baby inside of me. In the midst of the loss, I knew I had to say what is true about God and what I believed even in that moment. That is what I had to hold on to.

She gave her testimony that night, but the doubts continued. *What is God trying to teach me, she wondered. What did I fail to learn in my brain tumor crisis that I need to learn in this loss?* Heidi recalls a conversation with a friend that came at just the right time.

> My friend was checking on how I was doing a couple weeks after my miscarriage as we headed into our Sunday morning worship service. I confessed in a whisper that I thought God had taken our baby to teach me something I had failed to learn. With love and urgency, she grabbed my hands and told me that was not true. She reminded me of the love and care of the Lord, his nearness to me, and his purpose for suffering of all kinds. And through

> that tender moment and the mercy of the Lord, I believed. I believed that while I would always have more to learn and believe about my Father, he was indeed my Father. He was present and purposeful in his parenting and despite the deep loss of that child after a year of trauma, I began to take more faithful steps toward him that day.

Trusting Christ in the present, even with recounted blessings behind her, proved to be hard in that moment and in the years to come. Take any of the trials on their own—newly married, brain tumor, losing a baby, and then going on to have a full-term child—and it's a lot for anyone to handle. But as Heidi remembers, her strength and ability were spent. She knew nothing was possible in her own strength, God had to fill in what was lacking in her. And by his Spirit and his Word, he did. When she looked at her trial in the moment, it seemed impossible to overcome. But as she reflects on how God delivered her, and sustained her in the transitions and suffering, she sees that he gave her new hope to press on in faith.

When I talked to Heidi, I wanted to hear how God gives her belief now. She's walked through the valley, but how does this give her hope today? Heidi was quick to give credit to both God's Word and his people. Remember, in her lowest moment, it was her friends who spoke God's Word to her. It was God bringing to mind Scriptures that she could share with others, and that she needed on the very day her baby died.

> [Christ rejuvenates my hope through a] combination of God's Word, my dependency, and the people in my life. Some are in the same season as me, but others have a breadth of life examples. In having those conversations and having those friendships and interactions with different

> seasoned people, I see the same truth. (He doesn't change, and the truth doesn't change.) I talk with my young mom friends, and I talk with friends in different seasons who experience the same thing. The same with those who are older than me. It is a humble realization that these will continue to be a challenge. These skills and truths I've learned I will apply in a different way later.

Heidi still fights to believe the truth that it was not something she failed to learn or do that caused the Lord to take her baby. It wasn't a consequence for her unbelief.

These different hard things have opened doors for her to speak life into the suffering hearts of other women.

> In the positions that God has put me in with ministering to women, as a staff member and mentoring moms and teaching Bible study, gives me opportunity over and over again to give testimony to his goodness and faithfulness. I can relate to the mom who lost her baby and died in her arms. I can relate to the woman who is losing her hair from cancer treatment. I can minister to someone else, put God on display, and show him trustworthy.

Heidi hopes that as onlookers witness her life and how God has kept her through it all, they can also say, "If Heidi made it through, I have hope to make it through too; we have the same God."

When I asked her how she would encourage the weary Christian who can't see the end of the hard run up the hill today, she reminded me that suffering people need other believers to walk alongside them. They need them for the moment, but they also need them for the future. She said, "Today might be your hard time, but you will flip-flop who is in the valley and who is on the mountain top and on the path. Speak the same truths to each other." This is how Jesus gives us hope and proves he is someone to believe in. Yes, he has been through the valley first, going ahead of us. He's just the right person to comfort us when it's our turn and the road starts to descend. But he doesn't stop there. He uses his Word and his people to flood us with even more comfort, and then gives us the grace to do the same to those who are hurting alongside us.

Tracy's Story

There is a reason Job is in the Bible. In one sense, it helps suffering Christians know that suffering doesn't mean God has forgotten you—or is displeased with you. God is clear to tell us that Job was righteous. And yet, he suffered profoundly. I'm honored to share Tracy's story with you because she points to a persistent fight to believe, even when her circumstances point to unbelief. The consistent theme of Tracy's life is that God uses his people to restore our hope. The body of Christ are his hands and feet to broken and weary Christians.

Tracy's life is one of compounded trauma. She grew up in a home with an alcoholic and abusive father and a mother who was a nominal Christian. As a child, she was introduced to Christ by her grandparents and other believers. Her desperation led her to believe that there had to be a heavenly Father who would care for her family, despite all its brokenness. It took time for her to lower her guard to believe that God the Father was nothing like her earthly father.

As she grew older, her family moved to a new town to gain a new opportunity in life and to escape her abusive father. It was there that she found a church community and met her future husband. But her suffering only continued. After five years of infertility, she miscarried. Then when she finally gave birth to a baby, she had a second miscarriage eighteen months later, followed by additional infertility.

But the biggest blow came when she was pregnant with their third child. Tracy recounts this dark day in her family:

> On January 20th we woke up as normal and my husband played Legos with our four-year old as was their routine while I showered. My husband, Mark, then went to shower as we were off to a market. After a while I realized he had been in the shower unusually long and I checked only to find him slumped against the wall with hot water streaming over him. I called my mother-in-law who was a nurse, and she said as soon as she saw him she knew he was gone. Our world crashed around us in seconds. My little boy saw his father in the bathroom and wheeled out on a trolley, covered up. His first words were "Mummy, who is going to play Legos with me?" Later in the day he asked me if Daddy was coming back. I had to tell him the truth as gently as possible. Not being honest with him would have broken trust between us. I remember just saying, "Lord, I can't have a baby now. All my life I dreamt of a whole family loving each other and Jesus and now that's gone."
>
> We returned home [from vacation] broken, shocked, and unsure how to take one step at a time. As they had through every trial, our pastor and church family rallied 24/7, brought us food, sat with me and prayed with me, and people I didn't even know came to my door saying they had heard my story and wanted to gift me food

> or baby clothes. Three weeks after Mark died, I developed a very high temperature, pneumonia, a pulmonary embolism, PTSD, dangerously low potassium levels causing paralysis in my arms and legs plus premature labor at 32 weeks. My baby was small and not being nourished properly because of my health, but I was kept in high care and my family were called in because the doctors said I was not going to survive, and my baby might not either. But God. He had a plan for my life, and he saved my life and that of Lauren. Lauren was born at 35 weeks weighing just 2kg. I was warned there would be pipes and tubes all over her which could be scary, but my baby bean needed no pipes and tubes. Just an incubator for a day because she struggled to maintain body heat. God was right there in all that chaos.

Tracy's life continued to be stressful. Trying to care for a premature infant, while grieving herself. Single parenting for a little boy terrified his only living parent wouldn't survive.

Church became a place of healing for her, even as it also reminded her of her emptiness without her husband. Nothing could replace him, but eventually Tracy remarried and settled into life in a new church and with a father for her children. But the trials continued to come. In December 2023, she went for a routine mammogram and ultrasound. The results came back showing cancer.

Tracy's life seemed to turn a corner toward hope. Her daughter was getting married. Her marriage was thriving. She had never felt more fulfilled and settled. Yet years of suffering compounded, and she fell into deep depression. *Why does this happen to me and not other people?*, she wondered.

> A voice came back to me, "The difference is I am your Father and you are my child. You are not alone." Weeks of scary tests followed where I lay on big scanning machines rotating around me looking for cancer. But in every scary room I would ask God for a tangible sign that he was there. Sometimes I'd see a small light in the corner of a room with machines humming all around or suddenly out of nowhere a bird would sing and I would be reminded of how God cares for even the birds of the field, how much more does he care for me.

The same God who carried her through life in an abusive home, the loss of her children, and the death of her husband, carries her through this trial—even as it is ongoing. God's Word continues to give her hope.

> I began immersing myself in Psalms, Philippians, the story of Job, God's promises to Abraham, how Elijah suffered from depression, but God was always in control. I began Christian counseling, and again my church family and book club girls have rallied round together a prayer support group for prayer items and praise items along with meal schedules during my hard chemo week.
>
> I said to my husband yesterday that after each big life trauma I thought I knew God better, and on a level, I did. But today I can say I needed cancer to yield full control to God. I had insecurity issues and needing to be in control issues because so much of my life held no security or when it did, I lost it. There is true, unchanging certainty in the

> world and that is my God. He never leaves me nor forsakes me, and my cancer diagnosis has shown me this in ways I never fully understood.

Even in compounding suffering, Jesus keeps his people and satisfies them as the Bread of Life. He sustains them, even in wilderness seasons. He gets them through the pain of the hills and takes them to the other side.

CONCLUSION

The Stability of Our Times

Good Friday 2024 was a dark day for me. The church we served for years (and then abruptly left) was unraveling due to mishandling of abuse. I had spent months talking to law enforcement, survivors, and families affected by this trauma. Appeals to leaders for transparency failed at nearly every turn. One week prior, a bombshell was dropped, and one leader was leaving suddenly, his last Sunday was on Easter. All attempts for closure or reconciliation evaporated with his announcement. He was on his way out, even as the road ahead with arrests and legal battles loomed large.

We had been attending a different church for months, attempting to heal and find a new path forward. But when Good Friday rolled around, worshipping hardly felt good. I wanted to mourn. I wanted to grieve all that was lost for these survivors and their families. I wanted to lament the church's continued commitment to preserving optics instead of protecting the vulnerable.

We snuck into a back pew moving to the rhythm of somber music and guided by low lights. It was good to be there, remembering another dark day thousands of years ago. For most of the service, I choked back tears. I cried for the friends who barely recognized the church they loved. I cried for the survivors who weren't ready to worship again, let alone trust a pastor. I cried for the people I didn't know, sitting around me, wondering if they too were disillusioned with their faith amidst sadness and grief.

I cried for my children, confused by the constant movement from church to church as we tried to resettle. We were homeless, refuges in what felt like a foreign land—except the land held a shred of familiarity that made it even more confusing to them.

I didn't want to be there.

We collectively recited Scripture about the cross, betrayal, and grief our Savior endured on that horrific day when all his friends left him, and he suffered for our sin. And I realized I needed to be there. It wasn't enough to read about Good Friday on my own. I needed to experience it with fellow believers, even if I didn't trust them yet.

Toward the end of the service, I spotted an elderly couple a few rows in front of me. They couldn't stand—or at least didn't stand when everyone else was led to—so I missed them for most of the service. When we got to the last stanza of "Jesus Paid It All," their hands shot in the air, together.

> And when before the throne,
> I stand in him complete
> Jesus died my soul to save
> My lips shall still repeat
> Jesus paid it all, all to him I owe
> Sin had left a crimson stain
> He washed it white as snow.[1]

I was undone.

What gets people to the end, holding hands, singing "Jesus died my soul to save, my lips shall still repeat?" I could barely make myself walk through the doors of the sanctuary that Friday night, they shuffled in together—one with a walker, one helping the other. I don't know their names, but their faith anchored me. It carried me through a dark day. I imagine they have stories of God's faithfulness, but I imagine they have even more stories of their own dark days. You don't make it that far without seeing some things. You see loss and sorrow. You see joy and blessings. You see betrayal and heartache.

And you raise your hands to the same Jesus we've been looking at in John.

Last Man Standing

Of the four Gospels in the New Testament, John is the last Gospel written. He wrote this Gospel in AD 80–85, and Jesus died around AD 33. Consider all the events John witnessed in those fifty years after the death and resurrection of Jesus. He saw his friends die and friends fall away. He saw James martyred and Peter crucified upside down. He saw the church born and witnessed the Spirit descend on people from every tribe, tongue, and nation. He experienced church disputes, fighting over circumcision and the inclusion of Gentiles, and walked through the messy establishment of a new people of God. All the people he writes about in his record of Jesus's life are dead.

Of the apostles, John was the last one to die. And I wonder, were there times it was hard for him to believe too?

John ends his Gospel with these words:

> And there are also many other things that Jesus did, which, if every one of them were written down, I suppose not even the world itself could contain the books that would be written. (John 21:25)

Jesus did a lot more in his time on earth than John or the other Gospel writers tell us. What we have recorded serves a specific purpose—and as we've learned in this book, for John, that purpose is belief (John 20:31). John wants us to see, hear, and experience everything Jesus did in his life and believe in him. He wants us to see him for who he is and find life in him alone.

One of my favorite stories in Scripture comes at the end of John's Gospel. Jesus has just restored Peter after his denial. He has appeared to his friends post-resurrection, and he's giving them his final marching orders. He's going to leave them, just as he said. But he has a job for all of them.

As Jesus talks to Peter about how he is going to die for the name of Jesus, Peter veers over into the lane of John (who is walking with them), wondering out loud, in essence, "What about John though? If I have to die, what does John have to do? What is his mission?"

Jesus doesn't indulge Peter's question, instead saying, "If I want him to remain alive until I return, what is that to you? As for you, follow me" (John 21:22 NLT).

Peter wanted to know about his friend, but Jesus says, "Don't worry about him." John's journey involved him living into old age, exiled to the island of Patmos. Peter's journey led him to give his life for the name of Christ. At first reaction, Peter's end seems like the harder road. He dies a cruel death, hated for his allegiance to Christ. But John lived so long he was exiled alone. He lived so long he sees everything Jesus predicts come true.

Peter is dead by the time John writes his Gospel. John is the last remaining disciple, writing a theological reflection on the life of his Savior long after all his friends have died. He's seen it all—probably to a much more severe level than any of us have seen—and yet still believes.

It would be easy to doubt and give up for John. No one likes to be alone. In fact, repeated persecution is one reason people give up. It just hurts so much. But as one theologian writes, it's in these dark moments that we see him as someone to believe in.

> In the person of Jesus, those hungering for righteousness see his justice. Those thirsty for compassion see One who will not break a bent reed.

> Those battling doubt meet One who hears prayers to help our unbelief without judgment or shame. And those perplexed with confusion over the complexities of lies, and the fear of being lied to again, come face to face with the only One who is faithful and true.[2]

As the last man standing, that's what John tells us. He places us face-to-face with the One "who is faithful and true." In short, John isn't writing to us from an ivory tower when he introduces us to Christ in his Gospel account. He's writing to us from a place of suffering, from a place where all earthly trusts turned out to be either untrustworthy, disappointing, heartbreaking, or simply unable to last. And on the other side of that, his portrait of Jesus is clear:

> *In a world filled with ache for Christ to make things right, the preexistent Christ came to rescue us.*
>
> *In a world that cracks and shakes and changes its landscape faster and faster, Christ can steady you.*
>
> *In a world that demands perfect performance, Christ is not interested in your religious works.*
>
> *In a world that motivates people by shame, Christ has covered yours.*
>
> *In a world that is constantly thirsty, Christ quenches your thirst by his Spirit.*
>
> *In a world that always hungers for more, Christ satisfies you with himself.*
>
> *In a world that gives up on you or disappoints you, Christ exceeds your expectations.*

In a world that leaves you alone, Christ is with you as a faithful friend.

In a world that forgets about you, Christ prays for you.

In a world that takes care of only itself, Christ provides for you.

In a world that cannot cure human suffering, Christ offers resurrection life.

In a world of cruel leaders and wounded sheep, Christ is the Good Shepherd.

In a world that never feels quite right or safe, Christ makes a home for you.

And Jesus is not just that way for a moment, only to change the next. He is all of this and more for you *forever*. He has been these things for you in the past. He is these things for you in the present. And he will always be these things for you in the future. He cannot change.

"I know pain," John essentially says. "I understand the disillusionment and devastation that comes when you are let down," John laments. "But I'm telling you in every symbol I can reach for: he is someone to believe in."

Making It to the Top

We all want to be like John, right? Philippians 1:6 says, "he who started a good work in you will carry it on to completion." I want to make it to the end of my days reflecting on the believable Christ, even if I have a long history of unbelievable events behind me. But I only make it because he holds me, not because I hold him. If we learn anything from the Gospel of John, I hope this is it. He graciously gives us what he commands. He shows himself as someone worthy of our trust over and over again. And he gives us the grace we need to follow him and trust.

I'm terrified of heights. I don't remember when I realized this, but it's only worsened as I've gotten older. I'm also a mom of four boys who love hiking. So does my husband. We live near a mountain that even I can hike. There is a hard side and an easy side. The easy side of the hike can be done walking—like up a flight of stairs. The hard side requires you scale the mountain on all fours. I've never done the hard side.

Until one day I accidentally did.

Our family moved to a scenic side of the peak once we reached the top and as I attempted to hike back up, I realized the only way up was on my hands and knees. Somehow, I had moved to the hard side. One of my sons stuck with me the whole way (probably because he knew I would be scared), and on our hike up kept saying "Mom, it's so beautiful! Look how far we can see!" Even now all I can think about is the pit in my stomach as the wind blew and I thought I was going to fall off the mountain. In hindsight, I know that if a ten-year-old can do it, then it's not that dangerous. But thinking rationally wasn't an option for me in that moment. Putting one hand in front of the other was. I knew the top was just over the rocks, but my body screamed, "You may fall and die!" Did I mention I hate heights?

All I could do was think about the next step. If I looked to the right or left, fear overtook me. But when I kept my face toward the peak, and kept my breathing in check, I didn't panic and made it to the top.

I think that's what we need to do on the journey toward belief. Sometimes our path toward belief is climbing slowly up a mountain we didn't intend to climb. There are a lot of "what ifs" in the

Christian life. If we focus too much on what's on either side of us, we lose sight of the final goal—making it all the way home.

I started this book with the verse from Hebrews 13:8, "Jesus Christ is the same, yesterday, today, and forever." The Christ we've encountered in John—that list above in the previous section—is, again, the same today as he was yesterday and will be tomorrow. The man who preached that sermon I talked about from Hebrews is no longer my pastor, but Jesus is still the Christ—and he is still my Savior.

Throughout this book we've encountered barriers to belief. The book is not exhaustive, and I imagine there are stories I didn't capture and roadblocks I failed to mention. But I hope you found yourself in these pages. More importantly, I hope you found the unchanging Christ. There is, as another chapter in Hebrews says, a great cloud of witnesses surrounding you, cheering you on (Hebrews 11). Like that couple in the Good Friday service, they've found him faithful and made it to the end only because he kept them all the way.

I'm cheering you on too. There's a lot that makes Jesus seem unbelievable in this life, but he does not change even when everything else around you moves. So I put before you the same question John does: *Will you believe in him?*

Acknowledgments

I'M ALWAYS AFRAID WHEN I write these that I will forget someone. Books bear the author's name, but they also include a massive army moving the process forward.

I've loved this process working with Ashley Gorman and the team at B&H. Thank you, Ashley, for believing in the message of this book.

Don Gates again helped me navigate the world of publishing with his wisdom, experience, and ability to champion this project.

Whenever I read a book that moves me, I'm reminded that other people read it first to make it better. Justin Talbert provided theological and editorial precision. Winfree Brisley, Andrea Dockery, and Emily Tarter all read draft chapters and gave feedback. The book is better because of all of you.

Amy Rypkema kept me sane by her near daily audio messages throughout a hard year. Thank you for always being a sounding board for ideas, burdens, and Scripture references. I'm glad we can fight to believe in him together.

This book is bolstered by the women who shared their stories with me. We share a collective faith in a Savior who never changes. I'm honored to include their stories in this book.

My husband, Daniel, is a constant cheerleader, steady rock, and the one who holds our life together. He's also a ruthless and disciplined copy editor. We've fought for belief side by side through "many dangers, toils, and snares." Trusting Christ's grace will lead us safely home in the same way he's led us thus far.

Our prayer for our boys—Luke, Zach, Seth, and Ben—is that they would never lose sight of the hope that Jesus Christ is someone to believe in. We've seen him be faithful in the valley—may we see his faithfulness together all of our days.

Notes

Introduction

1. "My Hope Is Built on Nothing Less," written by Edward Mote, 1834. Public domain.

2. "Key Words in the Gospel of John," Monergism, accessed October 29, 2024, https://www.monergism.com/key-words-gospel-john.

Chapter 1

1. Trevin Wax, *Before You Lose Your Faith: Deconstructing Doubt in the Church*, ed. Ivan Mesa (The Gospel Coalition, 2021), 9.

2. When Paul calls Jesus the "firstborn of all creation" he is pointing back to Adam, the first created man. Christ is the head of Adam, above Adam, and does what Adam cannot do. He obeys perfectly, and unlike Adam, leads his "brothers and sisters" into righteousness.

3. J. Scott Duvall and J. Daniel Hays, *God's Relational Presence: The Cohesive Center of Biblical Theology* (Baker Academic, 2019), 24.

4. This is a theme they unpack in their book *God's Relational Presence*. They follow the entire story of Scripture from the view of God's presence, tracing it from Genesis to Revelation, and tying together key motifs and details.

5. D. A. Carson, "Revealing the Divine: Understanding God Through Jesus," The Gospel Coalition, August 18, 2023, https://www.thegospelcoalition.org/sermon/how-can-we-see-god/.

6. Andreas Köstenberger, *Signs of the Messiah: An Introduction to John's Gospel* (Lexham Press, 2021), 26.

7. Köstenberger, *Signs of the Messiah*, 27.

8. A. J. Swoboda, *A Glorious Dark: Finding Hope in the Tension Between Belief and Experience* (Baker Books, 2014), 205.

9. Charles Wesley, "And Can It Be, That I Should Gain?" 1738. Public domain.

Chapter 2

1. R. C. Sproul, *John: An Expositional Commentary* (Ligonier Ministries, 2009), 41.

2. The "credentials" idea is referenced in *Exalting Jesus in John* (Christ-Centered Exposition Commentary) (B&H, 2017) by Matt Carter and Josh Wredberg, 56.

3. Jim Davis, Michael Graham, and Ryan P. Burge, *The Great De-Churching: Who's Leaving, Why Are They Going, and What Will It Take to Bring Them Back?* (Zondervan, 2023), xxii.

4. Davis, Graham, and Burge, *The Great De-Churching*, xxii.

5. Davis, Graham, and Burge, *The Great De-Churching*, 24.

6. Davis, Graham, and Burge, *The Great De-Churching*, 27.

7. Davis, Graham, and Burge, *The Great De-Churching*, 28.

Chapter 3

1. D. A. Carson, *The Gospel According to John* (Eerdmans, 1991), 219.

2. *ESV Study Bible* Notes, *John* (Crossway Bibles, 2008), 2038.

3. Andreas Köstenberger, *Signs of the Messiah: An Introduction to John's Gospel* (Lexham Press, 2021), 58.

4. Köstenberger, *Signs of the Messiah*, 58.

Chapter 4

1. John Florio and Ouisie Shapiro, "The Dark Side of Going for Gold," *The Atlantic*, August 18, 2016, https://www.theatlantic.com/health/archive/2016/08/post-olympic-depression/496244/.

Chapter 5

1. R. C. Sproul, *John: An Expositional Commentary* (Ligonier Ministries, 2009), 177.

2. Mike Cosper, interview with Russell Moore, "Losing Our Religion: Russell Moore's Hope," *The Russell Moore Show*, podcast audio, July 26, 2023, https://www.christianitytoday.com/ct/podcasts/russell-moore-show/moore-cosper-book-losing-our-religion.html.

3. I want to be super clear here that I am speaking to people who have been hurt, disappointed, and even sinned against grievously by shepherds. You can trust the Lord, believe in the Good Shepherd, and work to see truth come to light. God has harsh words for bad shepherds. And in some instances, the law has harsh consequences for them too. Trusting that God will deal with sinful shepherds and seeking earthly justice through the legal system are not mutually exclusive. In fact, both are biblically faithful. You are trusting the Lord when you use his appointed means to bring truth to light. When a crime has been committed, the "sword" exists as God's instrument of justice (Rom. 13:4). When a pastor falls into sin that isn't a crime, church discipline exists to deal with his failing (Matthew 18). Both are God's mercy to the offended and the offender. And using these means is evidence that you trust the Lord.

4. W. Phillip Keller, *A Shepherd's Look at Psalm 23* (Zondervan, 1970, 2007), 18.

5. Keller, *A Shepherd's Look at Psalm 23*, 44.

6. As read in Keller, *A Shepherd's Look at Psalm 23*, 113.

Chapter 6

1. Andreas Köstenberger, *Signs of the Messiah: An Introduction to John's Gospel* (Lexham Press, 2021), 148.

2. Michael Reeves, *Delighting in the Trinity: An Introduction to the Christian Faith* (InterVarsity Press, 2012), 34.

3. Reeves, *Delighting in the Trinity*, 90.

4. Nicene Creed, https://www.anglicancommunion.org/media/109020/Nicene-Creed.pdf.

5. J. Scott Duvall and J. Daniel Hays, *God's Relational Presence: The Cohesive Center of Biblical Theology* (Baker Academic, 2019), 319.

6. James M. Hamilton Jr., *God's Indwelling Presence: The Holy Spirit in the Old and New Testaments* (B&H Academic, 2006), 99.

7. For more clarity on this verse, see "Glorifying God by Bearing Fruit in Union with Christ" by John Piper, February 3, 2014, https://www.desiringgod.org/messages/glorifying-god-by-bearing-fruit-in-union-with-christ.

8. J. T. English, Jen Wilkin, and Kyle Worley, "Bonus Episode: Union with Christ with Sam Allberry," *Knowing Faith* podcast, May 28, 2020, https://www.trainingthechurch.com/episodes/aae5r7azaa5nwx7-cgckw-3cj4n-bc8ne-pr4e4-emzrm-kg3hm-w29se-rdzll-7p8fb-fz2fh-63lf8-aw92r-gc3lm-rslbz-e2j2b-e4xyk-ykf9l-thnge-grbyl-dhs75-lh4ff-hm8s3-7gabf-9xtsx.

9. Michael Reeves, *Rejoicing in Christ* (InterVarsity Press, 2015), 93.

10. C. S. Lewis, *The Chronicles of Narnia: The Voyage of the Dawn Treader* (Harper Collins, 2004), 541.

11. Dale Ralph Davis, *The Message of Daniel* (The Bible Speaks Today) (InterVarsity Press, 2013), 57–58.

Chapter 7

1. Stuart Townend, "How Deep the Father's Love for Us" (Thank You Music, United Kingdom, 1995).

2. D. A. Carson, *The Gospel According to John* (Eerdmans, 1991), 565.

3. David Powlison, *How Does Sanctification Work?* (Crossway, 2017), 13.

4. Carson, *The Gospel According to John*, 566.

5. Powlison, *How Does Sanctification Work?*, 112.

6. J. T. English, Jen Wilkin, and Kyle Worley, "Episode 53: Up, Up, and Away (Acts)," *Knowing Faith* podcast, September 19, 2019, https://www.trainingthechurch.com/episodes/aae5r7azaa5nwx7-cgckw-3cj4n-bc8ne-pr4e4-emzrm.

7. Matt Carter and Josh Wredberg, *Exalting Jesus in John* (Christ-Centered Exposition Commentary) (B&H, 2017), 345.

8. Carson, *The Gospel According to John*, 568.

9. Carter and Wredberg, *Exalting Jesus in John*, 349.

Chapter 9

1. R. C. Sproul, *John: An Expositional Commentary* (Ligonier Ministries, 2009), 97.

2. Matt Carter and Josh Wredberg, *Exalting Jesus in John* (Christ-Centered Exposition Commentary) (B&H, 2017), 151.

Chapter 10

1. Rebecca McLaughlin, *Confronting Christianity: 12 Hard Questions for the World's Largest Religion* (Crossway, 2019), 194–95.

2. McLaughlin, *Confronting Christianity*, 205.

3. Dale Ralph Davis, "Unusual Savior," sermon on John 11:1–45, February 28, 2016, https://www.sermonaudio.com/sermoninfo.asp?SID=228161838581.

4. Tim Keller, "Truth, Tears, Anger, and Grace," The Gospel in Life, September 16, 2001, https://gospelinlife.com/sermon/truth-tears-anger-and-grace/.

5. D. A. Carson, *The Gospel According to John* (Eerdmans, 1991), 412.

6. Andreas Köstenberger, *Signs of the Messiah: An Introduction to John's Gospel* (Lexham Press, 2021), 202.

7. R. C. Sproul, *John: An Expositional Commentary* (Ligonier Ministries, 2009), 192.

8. Keller says the right interpretation here is that he's snorting like an angry bull. There is a rage to his tears.

9. Isaac Watts, "Joy to the World," 1719. Public domain.

10. Tish Harrison Warren, *Prayer in the Night: For Those Who Work, Watch, or Weep* (InterVarsity Press, 2021), 121.

11. Warren, *Prayer in the Night*, 123.

12. Oliver Hunkin, *Dangerous Journey: The Story of Pilgrim's Progress* (Eerdmans, 2016), 109.

Chapter 11

1. D. A. Carson, *The Gospel According to John* (Eerdmans, 1991), 489.

2. "The Effects of Homelessness on Family Stability," *Catholic Charities* blog, December 21, 2023, https://ccthin.org/news/the-effects-of-homelessness-on-family-stability?gad_source=1&gclid=Cj0KCQjwxeyxBhC7ARIsAC7dS38CZ-mzoM3KXU-k8iclPwKue2jcI6a39QixmdSCQ_cCmb_1ERncgJsaAqQvEALw_wcB.

3. Jen Pollock Michel, *Keeping Place: Reflections on the Meaning of Home* (IVP Books, 2017).

4. Mike Cosper, *Land of My Sojourn: The Landscape of a Faith Lost and Found* (InterVarsity, 2024), 39.

5. Russell Moore, *Losing Our Religion: An Altar Call for Evangelical America* (Sentinel Random, 2023), 150–51.

6. Martin Luther King Jr., "Meet the Press," April 17, 1960, https://www.youtube.com/watch?v=1q881g1L_d8.

7. Carson, *The Gospel According to John*, 487.

Conclusion

1. Elvina M. Hall, "Jesus Paid It All," 1865. Public domain.

2. Derek Rishmawy, "Take a Hard Look at Jesus," *Before You Lose Your Faith: Deconstructing Doubt in the Church*, ed. Ivan Mesa (The Gospel Coalition, 2021), 139.

Also Available

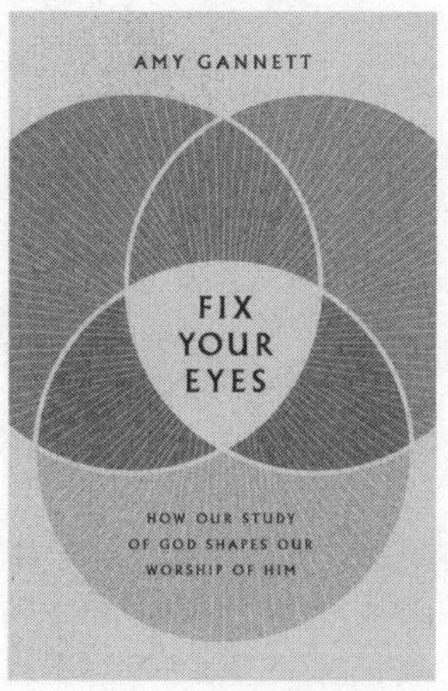

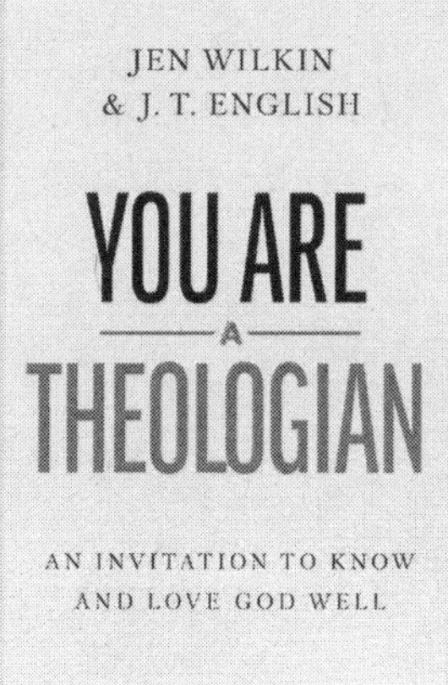